He was first selected as a regional winner and had his poem published in the book along with 250 other regional winners.

"All the winners get a free copy of this annual book and get to vote for what they think is the best poem in it," said Jenny Hodges of United Press. "The winner of the vote receives the first prize of £1,000 plus a magnificent trophy to keep for life." Nico received his trophy and cheque in a presentation at his local library in Bebington.

"It's an amazing competition and I would recommend anyone to enter it," said Nico. "I've written poetry for many years but never entered a competition before, and only entered the National Poetry Anthology at the suggestion of a friend of my mum."

"Anyone can enter the competition, and entry forms are available from most libraries, or people can enter via our website at www.united-press.co.uk, or by post to: NPA, United Press, Admail 3735, London EC1B 1JB," said Peter Quinn, Managing Director. "The aim of the National Poetry Anthology is to encourage more people to get involved in writing poetry and Nico is a perfect example. He was completely new to entering poetry competitions and has won at his first attempt. We hope he goes on to become even better-known as a poet."

Nico's ambition is to publish a book of his own work. As well as writing poetry, he enjoys writing comedy prose and is working on a sit-com.

"I've written poetry since I was a schoolboy, and most of my work is very emotional. In poetry you can express feelings in a far more intimate and creative way," he explained.

If you want to enter the National Poetry Anthology, submit up to three poems (on any subject) before the annual closing date of June 30th. There is no age limit to the competition, but you must be a UK resident.

Previous
National Poetry Anthology
Winners

2000 Louise Rider, Amersham, Buckinghamshire
2001 Ann Marsden, Saltburn, Cleveland
2002 Pamela James, Weston Favell, Northamptonshire
2003 Christine Masson, Sevenoaks, Kent
2004 Eileen Hudson, Rochdale, Greater Manchester
2005 Lawrette Williams, Drayton, Somerset
2006 Peter Button, Lancaster, Lancashire
2007 Stephen Holden, Preston, Lancashire
2008 Roy Lewis, Merthyr Tydfil, Wales
2009 Ed Collins, Southport, Merseyside
2010 Daphne Warrick, Milton Earnest, Bedfordshire
2011 Carole Bone, Glasgow, Scotland
2012 Nico Russell, Spital, Merseyside

Foreword

The National Poetry Anthology is now 15 years old and going strong. This particular teenager is bouncing with energy and enthusiasm.

When we launched the National Poetry Anthology towards the end of the Nineties it was just a "babe in arms". It was the germ of an idea for a free poetry competition which has now become the biggest free annual poetry competition in the world.

Every year we invite people of all ages from all over the UK - including Northern Ireland, The Isle of Man and The Channel Islands to submit their poetry.

Many of these are people who have only just moved towards poetry as a form of self-expression and a way of dealing with what's happening around them.

Others are experienced poets who have entered many times before and have finally, after years of trying, got through into the book.

All those poets - around 250 every year - receive a free copy of the book and get to vote for the best poem in it.

The author of that poem receives a prize of £1,000 and a magnificent trophy to keep for life. The presentation is made at the local library of the winner - chiefly because libraries are so supportive of this competition by putting up posters and handing out thousands of entry forms.

There are many ways of entering the competition - you can pop into your library and ask for an entry form or you can visit our website at www.united-press.co.uk or you can ring 0844 800 9177 or you can send up to three poems (no more than 25 lines each, including blank lines) to United Press Ltd, Admail 3735, London EC1B 1JB.

Peter Quinn, Editor

Contents

Each poet listed in this contents of the 2013 National Poetry Anthology is a winner in his or her own right. Their poems were selected as winners for their town or area in a free-to-enter annual competition. The winners are grouped into various regions. If you do not find a winner from your locality this is because insufficient entries were received from that area.

SOUTH WEST AND CHANNEL ISLANDS - Pages 64-88

Sassy Anne, St Helier, Kathy-Marie Stein, Truro, Kyla Sidwell, St Austell, Roland Gurney, Penzance, Joanna Pine, Plymouth, Gillian Balsdon, Exeter, Nels Rodwell, Exeter, Richard Kazimierowicz, Exmouth, Joanna Hatfull, Torquay, Beth Williams, Barnstaple, Jean Grimsey, Teignmouth, Sarah Boulton-Way, Plymouth, Pamela Joan Davies, Bournemouth, Kim Cannings, Bournemouth, P Radford, Christchurch, A Logue, Swanage, Christina Baxter, Weymouth, Ann-Marie Inman, Quedgeley, Sarah Bussey, Gloucester, Amanda Vizor, Cheltenham, John Clarke, Little Witcombe, Rachael Hewett, Weston-Super-Mare, Sandra Hobbs, Bristol, Anna Gillingham-Sutton, Bristol, Karen Rodgers, Chard, Norman Hutchings, Bridgwater, Heather Bonsall, Bath, Gillian Saunders, Bath, Beverley Bōrresen, Staverton, Helen Scull, Swindon.

EAST ANGLIA - Pages 90-101

Beryl Johnson, Cambridge, Marc Hollis, Peterborough, Karen Horn, Ely, John Brown, Peterborough, Ann Barnes, Meldreth, David Hill, Cambridge, Conor Beales, King's Lynn, Betty Fenton, Hunstanton, Marilyn Lucy Worship, Norwich, John Armstrong, Norwich, Joanna Sach, Ipswich, Hazel Thomas, Ipswich, John Harris, Bungay, Jasmine Ottley, Tuddenham, Stephanie Davies, Woodbridge, Luke Sayer, Newmarket.

EAST MIDLANDS - Pages 103-117

Ivy Moore, Glossop, Glen Mulliner, Belper, Emily Thomas, Youlgreave, Sam Monaghan, Hope Valley, Gillian Hartley, Repton, Julia Richdale-Ellis, Alvaston, Emily Hiley, Derby, James Cameron, Leicester, Michael J Guerrieria, Narborough, Stuart Morton, Oakham, OC Keens-Soper, Leicester, Megan Wood, Melton Mowbray, Maryse Smith, Lincoln, Barbara Donald, Scunthorpe, John Shillito, Barnetby, Suzy Holligan, Louth, Gillian Campen, Kettering, Matthew Musselwhite, Northampton, Audrey Smith, Hucknall, Kenneth Gear, Kettering, Georgina Youdell, Nottingham, Evan Gwyn Williams, Nottingham, Christine Proctor, Mansfield, Dean Geary, Retford.

WEST MIDLANDS - Pages 119-139

Ursula Mills, Hereford, John Kinross, Hereford, Caroline Ferguson, Bromyard, Tanita Keeble-Blaber, Oswestry, Ivy Willets, Brunt, Corinne Marbrow, Edgton, Josephine Bailey, Leek, Paul Holland, Stoke-on-Trent, Amy Dale, Meir Heath, Pete Hubbard, Burton-upon-

Trent, Jeanette Mckee, Ipstones, Marcia Phillpott, Rugby, Jackie
Smith, Rugby, Dave Brough, Southam, Rachel Stait, Sutton
Coldfield, Stuart Patnell, Coventry, Adeishe Hyera, Billesley, Alison
Hodge, Stourbridge, June McGuire, Coventry, Christopher Barker,
Walsall, Sheila Barnfather, Wolverhampton, Grace Mayne,
Wednesbury, Aliyah Begum, Birmingham, Louise Tapp, Berrow
Green, Gillian Reynolds, Shard End, Rebecca Shaw, Bringsty
Common, Lauren Stevens, Bromsgrove, Natalie Brookes, Redditch.
NORTH WEST And ISLE OF MAN - Pages 141-157
Alex Bell, Crewe, Andrew Muncaster, Macclesfield, Angela Johnson,
Chester, Ruth Evans, Middlewich, Anthony Payne, St Bees, Jamie
Smith, Stockport, Catherine Lee, Manchester, Hassan Imran, Bolton,
Rosie Garland, Manchester, Tanya Fernbank, Manchester, Rosie
Cooke, Rochdale, John Mcdonagh, Heywood, Brian Warren, Wigan,
Elizabeth Hart, Clitheroe, Jane Thornton, Oswaldtwistle, George
Palmer, Heysham, Anne Fielding, Ramsbottom, Yasir Hayat, Ashton-
under-Lyne, Judith Railton, Bebington, Alan Withers, Lytham St
Annes, William Potter, Liverpool, Susan Ironfield, Liverpool, Simon
Haigh, St Helens, Aidan Alemson, Douglas.
NORTH EAST - Pages 159-179
David G Dickenson, Hartlepool, Robert Reynolds, Seaham, Natalie
Crick, Bishop Auckland, Steph Acaster, Brough, John Liddle,
Consett, Luke Bowden, Hull, Freya Molineaux, York, Stacey
Quinlan-Smith, Kingston-upon-Hull, Sylvia Smith, Ripon, Rachel
Glass, Scarborough, Helen Weaver, Whitby, Daniel Gustafsson,
York, Sonia Mander, Richmond, Mikey Bambrough, Ashington,
Michelle Cadby, Alnwick, Yvonne Brunton, Doncaster, Christine
Stromberg, Sheffield, Judith Sanders, Rotherham, Carolyn Jolly,
Sheffield, Jean Hepton, Doncaster, Val Bolam, Newcastle-upon-
Tyne, Judith Magennis, Bradford, Paul Wilson, Newcastle-upon-
Tyne, Samantha Holmes, Newcastle-upon-Tyne, Christopher Craig,
Halifax, Ian Tomlinson, Leeds, Patricia Farley, Keighley.
NORTHERN IRELAND - Pages 181-182
Reza Ghahremanzadeh, Belfast, Paula Kennedy, Ballymena, Peggy
Galloway, Banbridge.
WALES - Pages 184-191
Heather Phillips, Nantymoel, Douglas Peachey, Swansea, Janet
Hughes, Aberystwyth, Sian James, Merthyr Tydfil, Dave Gallivan,
Swansea, Bernard Smith, Newport, Linda Jones, Rhondda, Beth

Richards, Gwynedd, Jill Berrett, Cardiff.
SCOTLAND - Pages 193-201
Bert Leitch, Glasgow, Norman Bissett, Edinburgh, Sam Reilly,
Giffnock, Kim Baillie, Edinburgh, Carol Habrovitsky, Glasgow,
Mandy Beattie, Wick, Vivien Heather, Inverness, Valerie Irvine-
Fortescue, Aberdeen, Ruth Miller, Fort William, Victoria Campbell,
Dundee, Greta Yorke, Prestwick.

South
East

13

COLD AND FROSTY MORNING

It's a cold and frosty morning
And everywhere is white
There'd been plenty of warning
From the clear and starry night

I feel the cold wrap around me
As I step out of my front door
The winter's setting in too quickly
It's almost chillier than I can endure

A delicate little spider's web
Usually hidden from my view
Today has crystals shrouding it instead
Letting me see its structure anew

I can see my breath as I exhale
Which is sufficient forewarning
That a cold wind will surely prevail
This cold and frosty morning

Julia Shepherd, Leighton Buzzard, Bedfordshire

WISHFUL THINKING

Thoughts woven tight like sinews of a drum
Twin stitched inseparable and then some
A friend spliced together at your side uniquely wondering
Warmly wanting reality's answer to fantasy's trade in

Daily I dare to ask why it should be such a task
Diligently acted out with sweeping smiles
Behind some desiring mask
A trend bedroom directed and exposed I suppose fully clothed
Of my pillow's secret thoughts no-one knows

Writing to reach you with words that besiege you
Even though they come from my mind
The pen to paper's embrace of my feelings mislaid in time
With finger contacts twitching
Emotion quivers in my face but then is gone without a trace

Destination 2012, some endless distance breached
It's time you believed in yourself enough to be reached
News highlights to please so many of whom you care
Click your heels, think a wish and just be there
Because there's something about this year that's yours to share

Steven Hibbs, Bracknell, Berkshire

THE GULL

Reaching our favourite seaside stall
We sit by the sea, whilst eating some prawns
There's a choice of seafood for us to eat
A perfect spot overlooking the beach

A solitary gull is standing nearby
Watching us with his beady eye
He looks at us and lets out a shriek
He struts up and down, his feathers so sleek

Why don't you feed me? He seems to say
Just a titbit and I'll fly away
We make the mistake and give him a taste
Then suddenly lands the whole seagull race

A girl and boy are sitting nearby
Eating their lunch - they don't hear the cry
Then on her lap a seagull lands
Grabbing her roll right out of her hand

Don't be deceived by these handsome birds
Grey and white feathers, and shrieks that are heard
Be wary if eating beside the sea
If they dive - cover your heads and flee

Margaret Cave, Slough, Berkshire

OUR LAND

When evening shadows cast their spell
Upon this magic isle
We'll gather friends and family close
To share a grateful smile

For all the good things in this world
Encapsulated here.
No need to travel far and wide
When everything is near.

Majestic mountains, rushing streams,
Quiet lakes and glens,
All the wonders of our wild life
Across the Norfolk Fens,

Dolphins off the Newquay coast,
Old Brock in his sett,
Red kites soaring high and higher,
Barn owl with owlets.

As well as nature's richest treasure
With which we are endowed,
There's our history and heritage
Of which we can be proud

Elizabeth M. Barlow, Windsor, Berkshire

KALEIDOSCOPE

Colours in my head,
Pieces of my life.
Intricately patterned,
Amazingly twisted.
Reflections in mirrors.
Where I came from.
What is my destiny?
Rapidly changing,
Loose coloured pieces,
Complex,
Convoluted,
A conundrum.
Fissions of colour,
Explode in my head.

Margaret Watson, Reading, Berkshire

THE GIRL IN THE WOOD

Whisper, whisper, the wind in the trees
The bird soars on the hidden breeze,
The trees with their tired old boughs,
Sing with the wind that runs through the clouds
The sun blares, adding heat to the scene,
As she perches on an old oak beam,
Her gaze piercing and at one with the wood,
The remainder of her face hidden by her hood,
The birds chatter out in warning cry,
She holds her place and out flows the lullaby,
The lullaby that prepares you for death,
Her hood is lowered as she readies her last breath,
She stares at the barrel that will release her soul,
Fear flashes in her eyes and she bolts as does the foal,
Yet she was no match for metal and gunpowder,
Her body broken until someone finds her.

Emily Fallon, Hazlemere, Buckinghamshire

THE PORTRAIT

With artist brush held in broad palm
No more precious time would calm
This feeling of most awful dread
As swelling thoughts filled up his head
Oft lingering perfume hung in the air
Hastening chills amidst lonely despair
This intermediate cold waiting phase
Before the portrait he could raise
On stark image free canvas sheet
Come quickly, oh bold creative heat
He was her keeper in flesh and tones
Mimicking rich peach covered bones
He owned her mind, deep heart and soul
To capture her essence now his goal
He swam in smell, colour, touch, delight
To shape form with a rare inner sight
Her portrait soon filled that empty place
Where before only thoughts would race
No longer in just imaginings but real
Her breath whispering as if life to steal
So she skillfully plied her artful trade
Whilst he with paint a portrait made

Jinty Pyke, Stoke Mandeville, Buckinghamshire

19

FROM THE BRIDGE

Come, my dear child and stand here with me,
On this bridge with the river waters tumbling far below
Just you and I and the bridge - the three of us
Here where the Roman once stood
When he was put in mind of another river
Et Thybrim multo spumantem sanguine carno
This time we will see again Cumbrian blood
For the Gelt rises in Pennine darkness
Made darker by a darker foe
Hold my hand and forgive us
For what our fathers ought to have done
Too late now
We Cumbrians are too kind
La vendetta é un piatto che non si serve
And now we wait here on this bridge
As the river of blood begins to flow
Sybilla ti theleis?
And the bridge answers as she did the Roman
Apothanien thelo

Peter Appleton, Aylesbury, Buckinghamshire

RAIN DANCES

When the rain dances steps of silver
In unseen ballet shoes
Hazy sunshine lights the fuse
Of waiting autumn hues.
As darkness snares us sooner
The light is strictly lunar
Yet I see you burning bright
By window, in candlelight.
As summer's body changes
Morning mist arranges
Orchards to explode
In colour with the sweetest scent
Where lonely traveller rode
And rain dances came and went.
Yes, the season still remains
When August hands the reins
To the grower of the grains
To welcome harvest for his pains.
We all reap what was sown
What you give is what you own
As rain dances on alone.

Kevin East, Chesham, Buckinghamshire

SIMPLE THINGS

Slowly and silently the lone teardrop of rain
Meanders a journey down the window pane
Creating a snaking pattern, trickling its way
Joining with more making a watery pathway

A poet finds words and inspires imagination
An artist paints a picture, a beautiful creation
An author creates atmosphere, within a book
To bring a read of pleasure when people look

Everyday events can be stored whatever way
Memories can be recalled any time of the day
A harsh clap of thunder and a lightning flash
Wet sand tickling toes as foaming waves crash

Watching the majesty of a cascading waterfall
And the emotion created by a game of football
Seeing the beauty of colour in a flower display
The magnificent sight of a train on an archway

Such simple wonders stored in books or frames
Are kept there forever to enjoy memory games
The world would be poorer without these things
Brief moments to relax when a happy heart sings

Margaret Cox, Milton Keynes, Buckinghamshire

SMILES IN MY EYES

If I had the power, at my command,
I would carve you a snowflake, in the palm of my hand.
I would craft you a bed, out of warm desert sands.
But there is no way to show my devotion,
Unless I weave you a dress out of the tides of the ocean.
And by making these things, my love would take form,
And I would give you a diamond, from the ice of a storm.
And if I could forge you a mountain, raise it up from the ground,
Just by raising my arm, without making a sound.
Then from that day, would brush upon your cheeks,
A white-gold earring, from its snow-capped peaks.
But even if I made these of land and sea,
You would be just as beautiful without me,
Because when I look up at the night sky,
Not a star holds a candle to the glint in your eye.
And when I look at the sunrise, and the night is exiled,
There is no such beauty as the last time you smiled.

Harry Radcliffe, Bourne End, Buckinghamshire

INTERMENT

The sunbeams filtered through the trees casting dappled muted hues
Over the gathered motley mourners meditating on a life well lived
A glad day in many ways despite Pat's life being cut short so cruelly
She was an agnostic as am I and many ad hoc collection of friends
But my anger burned and fluttered
At the clergyman rambling in haste
Saying the words
But clearly not feeling the reverence of the occasion
Time running short as another cortège was waiting in the wings?
Irreverence in this reverend is unforgivable despite my unbelief
When a vocation has become so routine that belief
Withers on the vine

William Keates, Southampton, Hampshire

23

JACK

He was a fire-cracker of a lad.
He filled the room with cheer.
He liked the company of men
And dominoes and beer.
Age twelve, into the mine he went
And worked with men who teased him,
Hid his snap, laughed and made him one of them.
Until the war upset all that.
He left his wife and kids to fight,
Although he could have stayed at home
And cut the coal from gleaming seams
To fuel the politicians' dreams.
And miners died beneath and on the ground.
They did not hear the bugle's sound,
The spur to die a glorious death,
With useless medals on the chests
Of children left behind, bereft.
But Jack survived to live again
To tend his greenhouse and surprise
With japs and incurves huge in size
And beat his mates in better wars
Where death was not the prize.

Audrey Dowsett, Gosport, Hampshire

THE WOMAN ON THE TRAIN

Oh beautiful woman
You heave and you sigh
Then silently dream
As the world passes by
What chance a kiss?
To whom does your heart belong?
Such tortuous bliss
While love weaves its song

As the journey ends
You wearily rise
The moment ascends
As I'm drawn to your eyes
Your smile holds me still
While my heart starts to dance
For your lips I would kill
As you start to advance

The warmth of your skin
And the draw of your breath
Your eyes pull me in
There is only you and I left
Then you pull back away
And leave with one final glance
But it's better that way
For the sake of romance

Simon Good, Farnborough, Hampshire

THE FINAL SEASON

Dark, dense days obscure the sun,
The plants all buried, dormant.
Violent storms attack the coast,
As Earth lies in her torment.

The bitter cold, the raining sulphur,
Eroding Nature's face.
Gentle giants in splintered carnage,
A sign of forgotten grace.

The scorched and blistered badlands,
Of solitude and void.
The delicate green and beauty,
Its balance now destroyed.

We did not heed the warning,
We did not share the love.
This time was no ark built,
No olive sprig from dove.

We erased our own existence,
And this we must accept.
Humanity's final season,
And Mother Nature wept.

James Cole, Waterlooville, Hampshire

NEVER QUESTION

Don't question why the world rotates,
I only know it's true,
And don't ask me why it's you I love,
I only know I do.

Ask me not why the sun comes up,
Or the moon at night,
Even why the tides rise and fall,
I only know it's right.

You may seek to question,
Why the Roman empire fell,
But no matter how you beg me,
The reason I cannot tell.

Einstein could tell you,
About time and mass and space,
Whilst on any question of gravity,
Newton was the ace.

Never question why my heart leaps,
When you are near,
No matter how I seek to tell,
The reasons are not clear.

Desmond Harder, Southampton, Hampshire

THE YOUNG SOLDIER

Golden hues of autumn painting
All the things my heart holds dear.
Red and gold the leaves are turning,
Whilst I lie and sweat and fear.

Fear that turns the night to terror,
And the day to smiling dread;
Fear that turns my limbs to water;
Terror pounding in my head!

Just young boys, we marched together,
With our hearts and voices high.
Now men lie in mud and water,
'Neath a terror-laden sky.

Here there is no past or future,
Here where hope is stained blood-red;
Gone the spring of youth's bright dawning,
Buried here amongst the dead.

But autumn leaves are turning
The forest to a flame.
In my home a fire is burning,
I may never see again.

Tereza Shortall, Aldershot, Hampshire

THE WORLD THROUGH MY EYES

Yesterday I was that girl that tiptoed through the flock of the nation
Behind those weeping eyes were hopes of celebration
Skin like caramel soon became the biggest frustration
The Lord's creation was an inspiration

Eyes darting as I walk through to the train station
The colour of my hair so dark, what a fascination

Today I am a woman that glides through the population
Through my fluttering eyes, seeing my future destination
That frustration has become the new perfection
This correlation between the Lord and me
Has become a strict legislation

Isolation emerged, feeling like a mock migration
The world through their eyes became an infestation
But the world through my eyes
Is simply another generation of a mixed exploration

Nurjhan Begum, Winchester, Hampshire

DOLPHIN

Calling high, gliding in a blue sonar symphony
Up, up, bursting in pure atmosphere from abounding depths below
Drawing in sweet air from triumphant spout
With nature's ever-trusting expectancy.
Salty glistening either side, as she moves on through the tidal stream
Without path or pilot, which only dolphin knows.
Testing time, fallible only by the nets which echo
With the ghost of her fellow being.
Yet smiling in her constancy, dolphin knows us
Transparent ever-changing
Lashing out at all that hurts, unlike us, silent eyes watch
And in her wisdom calm the very ions
Which shift the surf around her.
Dear to us for her playful companionable ways
Gently guiding conveying her praise
Take us back, dear dolphin, to that place in time where
All was a peaceful attunement of our minds.

Eileen Stockwell, Fareham, Hampshire

FEATHERED RAPTORS

In the garden and on the moor
Beware the flying predator.
The sparrow hawk is on the wing,
A silent killer; menacing.

Hovering high in static flight,
Swooping at the speed of light.
Beware, small creatures of fur and feather,
Hide beneath the grass and heather.
When its shadow is passing by
Death is lurking in the sky.

As night falls, out come the owl
From behind a chimney cowl.
On spectral wings it makes its flight
When the moon is shining bright.

Like a ghost ere the break of day
It seeks to feed upon its prey.
Beware small creatures of the night,
Keep well hidden; out of sight.

Maurice Daines, Isle of Wight, Hampshire

THE FRUIT PICKERS

They came in their blouses
From London townhouses
To work on the fruit farms of Kent

They came in their droves
To pick fruit from the groves
It was hard work but hours well spent

They came to earn money
And hoped it be sunny
As they stayed in tin shacks or a tent

Those fruit picking pickers
Who wore frilly white knickers
Those fruit picking pickers of Kent

Peter Neeves, Isle of Wight, Hampshire

THE ROSE

Velvet petals uncurl, unfold
Reveal their secret heart,
Wine-dark, pale pink and gold
Their fragrance lingers in the dusky gloom.

Luminous in the fading light
As darkling shadows creep,
Deepest blue and
The first bright star appears
To herald night.

Carol Rogers, Watford, Hertfordshire

HOME

I'm home. That red jacket of yours
Is strewn on my bed.
It fumes the room with your cologne
As if you are still stretched out somewhere under the sheets,
Ready to breathe me in again.

The sand in the shower
Has dried in curious waves in the tray
Where it fell from our bodies
And slid between our smiling toes.
Part of the night, heads on the shingle,
We felt the waves
And other things too.

But now we fall from each other again
For a little while.
The wind carries me home.

Francesca Platt, Knebworth, Hertfordshire

THEN, NOW AND WHAT THE FUTURE WILL HOLD

We are not logical,
No-one thinks of the bad in times of good,
Or the times of good in those that are bad,
We never think of the present,
The past is a dent in the bonnet,
And the future is a shadow getting larger and larger.

What is the present?
The past which we always think of,
Was always once a present,
And the shadow is getting bigger,
So black, dark and intimidating,
And when it comes, it's so unimportant,
And once again ignored.

Once the shadow has passed,
It becomes a dent in our memory,
Even though before, it was so scary,
When it was happening, it was nothing,
And whilst it was happening we were already frightened,
Of the next shadow, a small dot in the distance.

Stepan Mysko von Schultze, Hitchin, Hertfordshire

SENILITY

Sitting and staring out into space
A gash for a mouth in a wrinkled face.
Responding to little that goes on around
Eating and drinking, not making a sound.
Words all of a jumble, not making much sense
Locked in a body, a soul trapped by a fence.

Oh Spirit what makes these things happen at times
What is your purpose prolonging these lives?
Their loved ones are strangers, received with blank stares
No sign of recognition for this person who cares.
Oh, just once more Mum, if only a chat
They could go home happy, some contentment with that.

Now it's only a touch, that links with this being
That sits in the chair, eyes dead and unseeing
Sitting and waiting, who knows if it's soon
Will they survive to see next day's noon?
One thing's for sure in this withered old shell
A heart beating strong, suspends it in hell.

Adele Frost, Watford, Hertfordshire

THE UNCERTAINTIES

Is it that I am a fool for love,
Who is eternally trapped by Cupid's bow?
Or does your boldness intensify my mind,
And force my thoughts to never know?

Is the intimidation of a woman's beauty,
As genuine in appearance as that of Earth?
Or does it manipulate the essence of true life,
As a woman whose body fails to give birth?

Is potential as potent in the love of a dove,
As one who lives with the purity of lust?
Or is this conviction, when considered an addiction,
The divine limitation in the ability to trust?

Is this poem composed with embellishing passion,
And taken in meaning when helping one to cope?
Or were these jaded lyrics, when viewed as satiric,
Worthless as a beaten lung that pumps without hope?

Jamarcus Purley, Oxford, Oxfordshire

FRIEND OR FOE

Each of my steps unfolded the day
Glance oval greens and catch golden wheat
The undergrowth shuffle with delicate feet.
Crack branches, soft gentle breeze,
Bite the fruit and swallow the meat.

Each of your steps followed my way
Your hand reached mine and together we fell
The Earth folded us into its dark hidden cell.
Eyes closed, fully submerged,
Bite the earth, swallow the dirt.

Your hand still tight, you dragged me out
Caressed away soil and held me upright
Straightened my legs with your supporting weight.
Eyes opened, together survived
Bite the tongue, swallow the pride.

Elizabeth Philpott, Faringdon, Oxfordshire

FOREIGNER

In the inky darkness around the bed,
You lit a cigarette next to me, while
I followed the orange glow with dozy eyes.
Kissing me after, with a smoker's mouth,
Somehow, the coppery smoke tasted sweeter on your lips
Than on any of the others' and we fell into fitful sleep,
Your unknown body molten against mine.
In the morning I left,
Strangely smug at my non-achievement,
And walked home in yesterday's clothes,
In heels that moulded to last night's blisters.
Unsure of etiquette, sure in my autonomy
I left nothing: no name, no number.
But as I sit here, a part of me is missing.
Never too old for naivety, I thought we had
Both taken what we wanted in equal parts.
But, as I desperately try to assemble the jigsaw
And piece together the features of your face,
While your far-off foreign accent melts in my mind,
I realise just how wrong I was.

Emma Griffin, Henley, Oxfordshire

UNITED WE STAND

The call of spirit from deep within,
To the children of Scotland, it's time to begin,
To honour the dignity of the people in our land,
And take charge of our lives. United we stand.

Broken in spirit, downtrodden in heart,
The return of our stone is only the start,
Of healing the cruelties which tore us apart,
United we stand, with hands on our hearts.

Our strengths and our talents exiled from our land,
Have nourished the world with a guiding hand,
The seeds of our bloodlines, matured and now grown,
United will stand, in their spiritual home.

Divided no more by enforced separation,
By oceans or tides or imposed traditions,
Governed in wisdom, by me and by you,
United we stand, powerful and true.

As the force of spirit strides through this land,
Awakening hearts to what needs to be done,
Feel the rhythm build, like the beat of a drum,
United we stand, together as one.

Amara Michaels, Oxford, Oxfordshire

DARWIN DREAMS

Darwin finds
Time, summer 1859
To take his children and wife
For a few weeks break
On the Isle of Wight
Darwin works
In the boarding house
On the seafront, revising
The manuscript of the book
That book he will publish in November
Darwin paces
The beach each morning
Observing the waves, their sizes,
Their uniquenesses, whilst thinking
Through details, chapters, phrases
Darwin dreams
Of a beastly procession
A pandemonium charging from the ocean:
Amphibians, reptiles, mammals, birds
In packs, flocks, swarms, herds
Darwin wakes
And recalls his vision, his wife
Pets him back to sleep, as the gulls
Keep calling and the sea keeps lapping
Ever deeper into Darwin's ear

James Carter, Wallingford, Oxfordshire

CORMORANTS

Low-slung, slow long floundering flight
Heavy with black-winged weather
Only just over repressed and sulky water.
Dark, bulky portents maybe big-bodied threat of sea-change
Skimming the surface or maybe not.

Knotted on slime-aged rocks posed prehistoric sculpted
Against a seaweed sky eye-bright in watchful sentry stance
For sun's intrusion.
Pulled to sudden headlong lunging plunge.

And will the dead the sea gives up
Simply appear again
Calmly repulsed to life like these
Gloss-backed and surface-seeking souls
Here where they say the bells
From doomed and drownded townships
Sound? Who knows? Who knows? Who knows?

Colin Horseman, Colchester, Essex

I, ALONE

Worm infested grave tickles restless old bones
Aching for a comfort blanket of humanity to keep warm
Eternity to ponder where he went wrong, alone
Buzzing ground, hot underneath, the swell rising
Like an angry swarm

The burning sting, like a thousand poisonous arrow tips
Jolting decrepit leftovers into a dancing lunatic
Skinless hands tear through wood and earth
Like a devastating tide rip

The pain that lies ahead, adoringly apocalyptic
Vines grip tight, coiling like inquisitive snakes
Split skull rages in the darkness of night
Sobbing now at a wasted life, too late to shed the tag "reprobate"

The chilling sound forcing tree life to jump and take flight
Lord of the underworld stares into his soulless sockets
Crushing vice hold on neck bone, breathing fiery breath
The scorching flames open up his skeleton
Like a silver heart-shaped locket

The price paid in hell?
He gets to suffer over and over again, his own violent death

Chris Botragyi, Frinton-on-Sea, Essex

AN EVENING IN A WELSH BAY

The tide, moonlit and wrinkled
Crept silently, without malice
Along the sanded rivulets
That had been laid down by previous tides.
Time passed in slow motion parcels
Of moments and minutes.
Small fishing boats with sea
Shanty names bobbed endlessly
Rocking back and forth,
As the swell of crescent shaped waves
Ebbed and flowed like oil blackened velvet
Across a tailor's table.
And moonbeams folded and merged
Into white puddles of liquid translucent light.
And the people, my people,
Journey to warm coal-fired houses
With flames that flickered and
Licked at the darkness of the evening,
With a whispered welcome home.

Wayne Whiskerd, Chafford Hundred, Essex

SHE HOLDS MY HAND

She holds my hand,
And as she looks into a past
Grown muddled by confusion,
I see the glimpse of a wistful smile
Curling her trembling lip.
She and I, though fingertips apart,
Are separated by memories.
Hers, of a time, when young and vibrant
She spent her halcyon days intoxicated
By the joyous perfumes of youth and freedom.
Mine, of a time, when laying cradled in her arms,
I wept at the prognosis
Her, not understanding what lay ahead.
Me, grieving the death of a soul still living
In a fractured world of forgetfulness.
I study that face, so familiar
Yet so unrecognisable.
The light of a passionate spirit
Smothered by shadows of uncertainty,
Leaving ashes of fear, desperate vulnerability.
Behind us, the rays of a slumbering sun
Cast a halo of innocence around those silver tendrils
That gently frame her wrinkled brow.
And I am caught breathless with love
For this mother - child of mine.

Nicky Cox, Brentwood, Essex

MARRY ME

Beautiful orchid
Blossoming in the evening sun
Sand dunes whipping in my hair
Skinny-dipping in an ocean of blue
As crystals of sugar melt in my mouth
Throwing you down onto a blanket of blossom
I tell you how I want to spend the rest of my life with you
A twinkle glowing in your eyes
Like the Eiffel tower lit up at night
Scaling new heights

Jeremy Warder, Twickenham, Greater London

THE SOLDIER

He hath nothing left now,
But still he keeps his pride,
His friends are long forgotten,
But his rifle's by his side,
Poppies bloom around his feet,
A sign of all he's lost,
He's scared to die, but still he knows,
He must fight at any cost,
And he sheds a silent tear,
For his family, lost in the Blitz,
Buried and covered whilst he was at war,
His life slowly crumpled to bits,
And he prays for his wife and his beautiful son,
With bright eyes and soft, curly hair,
And he runs with his rifle, to live or to die,
Hoping soon he will join them up there.

Jessie Whichelow, Wimbledon, Greater London

THE SCENT OF BUDDLEIA

Ladybird, ladybird, crawling so slow up and down
The sealed window of this air-conditioned, office tomb.
How did such a lovely bug as you
With lustrous, orange wings, black-spotted
And exquisitely folded, get trapped inside
When sultry summer swoons outside.

Even here, in the city, are signs of its stay,
However temporary that may be.
Orderly squares with close-cropped grass,
And uniform flower beds under firm control
Of professional gardeners, peeved to see
Random weeds, shooting up unrestrainedly,
Riotously, and far too impudently,
Between the joins of paving stones.

In a matchbox at lunchtime I'll carry you to the river,
To an abandoned building not far from the tower.
And there release you on a scented bough
Of purple blossom buddleia, burgeoning,
Running wild in the long untended, tangled garden.
Later, back in the air-conditioned, office tomb,
The lingering, heady scent of buddleia on my hand
Will, I fear, disturb and distract all the afternoon.

Lynne Munn, London, Greater London

LITTLE DID I KNOW

Little did I know
Life would maze thousands of questions
Without me knowing the reason
I'm expected to summon
Shrouded by heat of the sun
Drenched by the frostiness of the rain
I breathe, I heave
Little did I know
Love would galore my heart
With pain and numbness
Without me having its solution
I'm expected to live
Clouded by the gloomy face of the sky
Shadowed by the taste of loneliness
Life cargoed many surprises
Across the coast everyday well sealed
One of them is adversity
That fling us to sniffles and sorrows
Little did I know
All of a sudden joy melts into pain
To develop countless tears
Without me knowing how to bring a smile
Little did I know
One day through it I would have to go

Shazia Ameerun, Enfield, Greater London

SNOW ON TREES

Winter's green splendid beauty spawned
Freshly-pure bright a soul dawns
Duly-treated speech tested
Freshness ice-cold raw
Green-love flurry time's besotted
Verdantly white or lily-lime thaw
Tepid light arises beyond conical forms
I linger, staggered and assured

Sydney Parker, London, Greater London

ABSTRACT CRAFTSMEN

The metal workers tap their hammers daily
Shaping the sharp edges of their letters into labour
That creates the chains and rings in connected threads.
These smiths of words in factories of homes and offices
Before the milled machines, they forge their meaning
Not dissimilar to hot press newspapers of the past.
But instead of lead, the electric impulse bleeds
Into the ether with the ghosts of chattering
On social networks and the coins of commerce
Flow invisibly in fictitious lines.
Bills are paid as a button's pushed
And reality is a mere transaction no-one senses,
As gold and silver is simply this century's common ore.
But the wires are molten, heated, tangling
In the talking fingertips that pulse and beat
The soft stuff of nothing hoping to transmute
From the computer screens of dreams
Day and night with keys unlocking gems
Into necklaces of wide-eyed moons and falling stars.

Bart Wolffe, Coulsdon, Greater London

WHAT IF

Something awful has just happened,
And those words enter your head,
You think about them again and again,
As you lay silently in your bed,
In the morning they're still there,
Guilt is feeding off that phrase,
Thinking back into the past,
Considering different ways,
But it is impossible to change,
What has already been done,
But don't give up because you know,
That your guilt has not yet won,
Disintegrate those silly words,
Because they cannot help you heal,
Swallow all that useless guilt and,
Express how you really feel,
Two words can influence your thoughts,
Don't let them control your life,
Or let guilt control your emotions,
As you'll begin to live in strife,
What if is a silly phrase,
It cannot change the past,
So push it out of your mind,
And you'll be at peace at last.

Charlotte Beaumont-McAllen, Rochester, Kent

ECHOES FROM THE PAST

A circular track around the field
Its grass in long need of a cut
Lonely figures waiting
Where bats once held rule
Desolation marks the spot
Where once there had been a ball

A circular track runs its silent course
Where once were games now lies remorse
Now only weeds are waiting
Where racquets once scored an ace
Nets decay in their own good time
Of the pits that once were jumped
There's now so little trace

Crows patrol these lonely paths
Where hurdles once stood high
Upon the fields where javelins flew
Only pigeons take to the sky
The silent cries of happy kids
Just echoes from the past

Kevin Andrews, Ashford, Kent

REMEDY FOR INSOMNIA

On such a night when sleep will not come
And darkness is close devoid of breath,
When morning seems more than a lifetime away
And a score of worries nag me half to death,
I recall childhood days at the height of Summer,
Of gold diamonds reflected on sun-latticed leaves,
Watch the wind as he chases threads of quicksilver
Through copse after copse of whispering trees.

Feel again the sun's heat through cotton clothes,
Hear the sensuous song of sun-soaked crickets,
Sense the sharp prick of sand between sandal and toes
As I thread my way through heather thickets,
Stars of sunlight sparkle gold sequins on water
Where ripples glow from the smiling sun,
Relive the delight and warmth of the shallow lake
A child's paradise for a day of enjoyment and fun.

Soon, gold-tinged leaves merge with sun-right water,
The lazy lisp of insects lulls me to sleep,
I drift away on clouds of perfect comfort,
A contentment of bliss and perfect peace.

Pearl Davis, Maidstone, Kent

AGE

Crumbling, curved spine tingles terribly.
Downy hair wilts to wintery white.
Slipper bites into swollen feet.
Voice croaks through yellow-coated teeth.
Mottled hands of creased brown paper.
Gown garnished with moulding memories,
Fairytale beginnings finally forgotten?
Wedding cakes and pumpkins long since rotten.
Tiara rusting in the bottom drawer,
Cinderella had no idea what was in store.

Lucy Beech, Gravesend, Kent

A MERMAID

Your hair tossed the water about you,
Weightless waving,
As your carefree face smiled a league.

Under sheets of emeralds,
You danced.
Together you banded krill, porpoise.
The killer whale stopped his strike
To study your graceful twists and turns.

For all of us mortals,
Mingling about,
Lying up in the sanctuary of undiscovered caves,
An ocean's life-time consistency,
Currents, tides and the moon's many faces,
See you perfectly reflected.
Immortally made as diamonds.

Zara Howard, Haslemere, Surrey

THE BROKEN CHINA DOLL

There sits the broken china doll.
Time has really taken its toll.
Chalk-white face, brown hair,
Pale blue dress with a little tear.

Memories of children giggling,
And of mothers with their fingers wiggling.
Then they'd grow up and throw her in the bin.
The bin made of cold, hard tin.

Then the cycle would begin again.
Until she was lost in a garden den.
Forgotten and alone.
Broken and alone.

Kimberley Flux, Maidstone, Kent

A BUNCH OF DAFFODILS

The grey streets rain endlessly
And the clay men in their beige coats
And dripping black umbrellas
Look more washed out every minute.

I cradle my bunch of daffodils
And they smile brightly in my arms
Spilling their gold onto the pavement
And drawing the weary passing eyes.

I see the light of my daffodils
Reflected in the nameless faces
And gently I too begin to smile.
The people now look at me.

Gillian Harris, Guildford, Surrey

DAMNATION

I travelled beyond the moors one night,
Lured by silver slivers of moonlight
Heavenwards I was dragged,
Struggling as warm hands bound, gagged
And set me in wax to live an empty death.
All and nothing escaped me.
Left voiceless, I began tearing at those emerald eyes
Of hated angels, giving them no choice
But to hurl me down from the skies,
Possessed again by my icy breath.

We embraced in a death-grip, at last.
We grow together: a great oak, He and I,
My pillar of the universe, fixed, steadfast;
Drowned in treacle darkness, the soil bled into my
Bones, the eternal rocks beneath.
I watched a soft-faced moon
Orbit around me, pulling my water's surf;
But he rends me open, a scorching demon-dancing fire
Breathing me into himself. He encircles me and I Him:
We are each other's hellish, haloed wreath.

But it is my white-hot heart that bursts and ignites
Its ashes scattered on the eternal winds of
Wuthering Heights.

Amber Gibson, Sutton, Surrey

MATINS

One cold morning, when a thin mist
Slipped over the rooftops,
A small bird sat on a chimney and sang,
A tiny dot in the blank, grey sky.
Cars hissed past, and racketing lorries,
But still he sang,
A song ten times larger than himself,
Then suddenly was gone.

May Worthington, Woking, Surrey

ARRIVING

Here comes the tardy train, slinking aside the platform
Full of embarrassment and cross commuters.
We stand at the edge in a reception line
Like relations at a wedding, only less well-dressed.
The train squeaks its apology and moves no more;
The doors whisper open, the weary tumble out, the young,
Like bounding balls, lollop down the steps, and middle-aged ladies
Gingerly edge out on spikey heels which barely bear their weight
Down Oxford Street, through Piccadilly, Fortnums, along
The Embankment to the Tate, and then, at last, Victoria.
Ah, yes, Victoria! The sirens and alarms, the tannoy messages
And police patrols herding the hopeful passengers away from trains
To which they're crowding, eager to be home.
Out come the mobile phones, tired cheeks are sprinkled with fresh
Tears, while hefty, briefcased men stampede around, and swear
And blame the government.
Hours late, but here you are, and now I lead you to the waiting car
And home, safe from the terrorist, but back to a computer crash.

Sylvia Herbert, Fetcham, Surrey

STRAWBERRY RONDEAU

At Strawberry Fair they thread their hair
With fabric flowers bright as air.
Beneath a sky that can't be wider,
Graceful as a tie-dye spider,
I watched a lady dancing there.

Her henna-tattooed arms were bare,
And she had yards of skirt to spare,
That swept and flowed and leapt to ride
The music synthesised inside her,
At Strawberry Fair.

More like epiphany than prayer,
And more like lucid than aware,
Every blade of grass described her,
Hair like coffee, eyes like cider,
On the beating field we shared,
At Strawberry Fair.

Marc Thomas, Brighton, Sussex

SHADOWS

The beautiful tragedy of light on a graveyard,
A seeping silence of endless nights,
The fairy who dances through thoughts of her weeping
And thrives upon her stinging tears.

She shrieks and she laughs as she breathes on her neck -
The madness of time ebbing away.
Sensing fear, the fairy, with claws on her hands,
Coaxes demons from the moonlit air.

It's evil, it's nonsense, it's haunting all thought,
But she's bleeding and frantic, unsure.
If she tears out her demons then what will be left
But empty, lost feelings and scars?

Marguerite Christine, Chichester, Sussex

MEECHING DOWN

Snow fell on icy snow
Silencing Meeching Down
Seasoned crows and jackdaws dotted the crystal landscape
And plump wood pigeons perched high in the surrounding trees
No four-legged creatures were in sight
But their footprints were clearly visible
Intriguing paw marks
Large and small
Punctured the snow
There had already been talk of a cat
As large as a panther
Roaming nearby
And now the local 'rag' confirmed a sighting -
How exquisite

Jennifer Jones, Brighton, Sussex

57

VIEW ACROSS THE PARK

Through the branches, through the leaves,
Ripples blown by the breeze
Gulls are coasting up and down
On their watery merry-go-round.

Bluest blue of summer skies
Blossom waving, gulls squawk cries,
Circling, banking up on high
Time is drifting, dripping by.

Ensconcing warmth, the summer sun
Wrapping, holding, healing one,
This view unchanged year upon year.
Yet child on swing now disappears ...

Its constancy, part its appeal
Always the same, its timeless wheel
Of seasons, nature to observe
Each and every tiny bird.

Sue Goodall, Bexhill-on-Sea, Sussex

A UNIFORM PROBLEM

Class 3D were very keen,
The brightest class you've ever seen,
But school uniform they hated,
Their teacher was exasperated!

Do you think it's right Kiara,
That you are wearing a tiara?
Madeleine, take yours off too -
Oh my gosh, is your hair blue?
Bob, those roller blades are great
But walk around school, please do not skate.
And Mary Jane, is there a reason for sunnies
In this winter season?
Jack, I don't want to see you twirl;
Take that skirt off, you're not a girl.
And Sophia, as for you,
Those lime green tights just will not do.

I want full uniform tomorrow,
I don't care how - beg, steal or borrow,
I would really like to see
Every child as smart as me.

But Miss, Class 3D loudly said,
You wear your knickers on your head.

Melanie Jackson, Crawley, Sussex

VENUS PERCEIVED

How pleasing to walk
On a cool dark night
Away from cities or towns.
To gaze at the stars, see
The moon rising.
Contemplate within your soul
In perfect peace and quiet.
Have the added pleasure,
To see the brightest star in the night
Venus - Earth's sister planet
The Babylonians thus named her.
For they too were smitten,
Centuries ago
Nothing can be so overwhelming
As viewing the Canopy of Starlight.
Such an experience remains,
Forever in the human mind.

Joan Iveson, Peacehaven, Sussex

ON THE EDGE

Fake Neddie Seagoon orchestra dramatic mysterious chords
Playing crazy music that lit up his brain
Like a demented ape
Longing to escape
From this locked-in place.

Space, space
Mystery in tune with something
Maybe the moon.

They say the moon can affect you that way.
They say when it's full, the pull
Can take you into dark places.

He's dancing now like an African tribe, curing manic depression.
Dancing till he drops.

Into sleep and peace
Music fading.

Locked-in place, place locked in
A long life, but still with places in-locked
Traces of freedom, daring to bring to light
To plain sight a new expression.

Turn the key,
See with new eyes
Descaled.

Jean Wagstaffe, Eastbourne, Sussex

ANTI VANDAL PAINT, STRONG WINDS AND STRONGER LAGER

Fresh air, without a care,
Windswept,
Unslept,
Bedded down,
We invent a town,
Invent a place,
Invent a meaning,

Then through lack of aim,
And bows 'n' arrows we can't tame,
We try and fail to re-invent,

With our times money spent,
Just whittled away dreaming,
We'll just sit 'n' settle, on a simple, easy, half-hearted feeling,

Never again!

Macus Hillier, Bognor Regis, Sussex

South West

APART

Seraphic complexion and crushed berried mouth
Loosely laced with an unsullied smile
Softly woven with powder light scent
Leaving sweet dewdrops wherever she went

His grazes like thistle his cracked labourer's hands
Curled up mementos of lost ambition plans
Bark knotted finger beckons her down

Fantastic fantasies furl through her fire
A direct order is all he has sighted

Soured breath
Eeled cock-sure to the treasure nest
Her beauty now only as good as the rest
As like a sand flea on nitrated shores
He hovers and jumps for the tastiest bits

Spartan and strict with simple disclosure
He hastens the moment which sorely broke her
Now berry to wine and powder to clay
Subtlety and suppleness are buried to lay

Sassy Anne, St Helier, Channel Islands

ICARUS

Tell me, what were your desires,
Curiosity, strength or happiness?
Were you unearthing the waxy boundaries of life,
Or battling some unconscious strife?
O share the wonders of your heart's enchantment.

Take me up so I may charm the seagulls,
And dance with the soaring crows,
Show me how to make my father proud,
I too wish to dance in the wild blossoms
Of man's emptiness.

Kathy-Marie Stein, Truro, Cornwall

REFLECTION DISRUPTION

Do you see me in that window?
And like me does it not stray beyond the glass?
The oasis of wavering bodies
Carpets a landscape of pattern
That travels and you with it;
Twisting among the pile - and there behind you
A thing, sticky, globular and beguiled.
A blink of trickster dust in my eye;
I am sorry but not still.
The white clouds, bleached and toned pass,
Exercising their right to lie.
You lean towards and past the glass,
Rippling the reflections and this solid face -
Only a scream can erase.

Kyla Sidwell, St Austell, Cornwall

NIGHT

We breathe in the day's belated death
Through open windows inviting in the night
Prowlers parading around our green gardens,
Rabbits, foxes, badgers, moles, mice and the odd rat.

Above the rich nocturnal air floats
A full moon like a snow white bare breast.
Mounts Bay appears brimming with ghostly armadas,
Remains of shipwrecks and all night fishing boats.

Our black dog listens and sniffs for every sound and scent.
Mid-afternoon he swam ten times in Halamanning lake,
Cruising in effortlessly like an olympic gold medallist,
His cool wet fur glistening in the heat-haze bake.

I still feel the grandslam impact
Of this morning's melancholy fist on my heart's full face.
Now Mozart's Serenata Notturna so stark and beautiful
Can't stem my bolting blood's clamouring for the dark.

Roland Gurney, Penzance, Cornwall

SIXTY

One thinks of crones
As skin and bones
With witchy pointed hats
Long frizzled hair
Clothes of despair
Surrounded by many cats
And then there's me
And you can see
I do not fit the bill
My form is round
My clothes are sound
And *one* cat sits on the sill

My hair is neat
It is a treat
And my hat is oh so twee
I've joined the ranks
And I give thanks
For the crone that is now me
And so dear friends
I'll make amends
And thank you one and all
Deep from my heart
And before we part
I'll wear the purple shawl.

Joanna Pine, Plymouth, Devon

TULIP POWER

Oh floral carpet that covers Holland,
With your seas of red, like unquenched fire,
Rise up triumphant and touch God's hand,
And bloom eternal to your heart's desire.

With your oceans of yellow, that shimmer with gold,
You pour contentment from tall chalices,
In pride and glory your beauty unfolds,
And light the way to celestial palaces.

Gillian Balsdon, Exeter, Devon

PLAYED ON STRINGS

With these words - I'm going to say
For what it's worth - to you
Melody - an easy tune - played on strings
For what it means - to you ...

The time we've had - seems like a single day
Hold onto me now - we're minutes away ...
You can go now - I'll stay
Playing on strings - smile your last breath away ...

I know there's nothing that I can do
I feel I belong with you
It is what it is ...

Left - with your things
I can only stay here for so long
Before life moves me on ...

Nels Rodwell, Exeter, Devon

IT'S TIME

Grandfather in bed, granddaughter at his side
She looks at his face in the flickering light
His eyes twitching like the candle, their fates are tied
An inch of wax, end of the road in sight

The pendulum beat that was once so strong
Falters with a weak and irregular pulse
The key that powered this man for so long
Has lost its ability to impulse

The creaking case that holds the motive force
Is strewn with cracks and variegated flecks
Over many years the structure has been reinforced
But now the joints are akin to shipwrecks

Eleventh hour gone, midnight chimes start to ring
Her tears tick-tock onto her grandfather's hands
The wheels have stopped turning and it's time to bring
To rest, the hourglass sands

Richard Kazimierowicz, Exmouth, Devon

CAMOUFLAGE CAT

Upon the ink-stained sheets,
Still and quiet,
I bend down to tie my lace.

Flashing past so very fast,
A glimpse of jet black fur
Illuminated by a pair of piercing orbs.

They burn brighter,
Like lamps they light up the street
And before me she trots

Her silent paws pad the pavement
And her full form
Comes into view.

And then she vanishes
Once more
Swallowed by the night.

Joanna Hatfull, Torquay, Devon

UNWANTED GUEST

A girl sits down by my nest,
She looks at me horrified,
She tenses up,
I can smell her food,
Honey, chocolate,
I want it,
If she won't share, I'll sting her,
She looks warily at me,
She shuffles up,
I walk on and stop by her side,
She drinks her tea, I'm so thirsty,
Sweetness,
She is the first child who hasn't tried to kill me!
I buzz,
She screams,
She goes,
No friend for wasp.

Beth Williams, Barnstaple, Devon

PATERNAL LOVE

I only went to mass to be with him,
Once a year, maybe twice,
It was the only time we were alone together.
I drove him to his church
Where, as the oldest member of the congregation,
He was respected and revered.

But I was like a child again,
Moving automatically through genuflection,
Head bent and covered, breast beating, whispered prayer.
I lost myself in the smell of incense,
Sound of hymns, resounding silent moments,
And long-remembered words.

There is a point within this modern mass,
Where neighbour turns to neighbour with the sign of peace.
Most clasp hands, a smile, a murmured greeting.
My father opened wide his arms,
Gathered me in and held me close,
All accepting, all forgiving.

Jean Grimsey, Teignmouth, Devon

72

WATER COLOUR

Sweetest rain so warmly graced
Every hue upon her face,
Beauty's silks ne'er runneth down,
Not a line in fret or frown.
No deep shadow, no cast shade
Can e'er eclipse this golden glade!
Silhouette of whispered flight
Paint the Sistine of the night.
Dorian not covet me,
Pure of heart her passion be.
Guernica no weeps its lease,
Portrait weaves her kiss of peace.
Monet melts the mood as she,
Awakens parasol in me.

Sarah Boulton-Way, Plymouth, Devon

LEAVE-TAKING

She held the precious bird
Feeling his steady heart beating
As she carried him to
A distance where he could
Float on the thermals,
And in the calm light of day
Would discover his true course.

It was time to leave,
She opened her hands with care, then
With an upward movement
Of her entire body and arms she released him,
And he was on his way
Leaving the girl with laughing eyes
Watching until he was a speck in the distance.

Pamela Joan Davies, Bournemouth, Dorset

THE SPECTRES

People starving by their billions.
Developed countries hand out their millions.
To salve their consciences, I assume.
If we would only a little less consume.

Concave legs and convex bellies.
We see it all on our tellies.
Of our lifestyle we may groan.
But of such suffering we've never known.

Another woman crying at her dead man's feet.
Her provider gone, baby at her empty teat.
War is the cause, the evil rule prevails.
What counts in the end, are armament sales.

So tell me, please. Must they suffer their lot?
And can someone explain, where is their God?

Kim Cannings, Bournemouth, Dorset

THE HERON

Motionless he stood,
His two thin legs mud-planted
Safe, in the calm waters
Of his reed domain.
Back stooped as aged man.
Scanning with translucent eye
The weed green depths below.

No breeze his plumage stirred,
As grey on grey the coverts line
The perfect symmetry of form,
Seeming moulded by a potter's thumb
And set in some paludial land.

Yet as I watched, transfixed as he,
Time held within that little world
His long thin beak with laser speed
Slivered that tranquil scene,
As gorged with innocent fry
He rose majestically, his great wings arched.

P Radford, Christchurch, Dorset

INCOGNITO

Pretending we were a mystery
Feeling that we might be heading off
For another adventure,
Who would know anyway?
There is nobody left to sing our song
Save us, we are the last survivors in love.
We clutch and fumble at each other
Hands and luggage,
This is a new venture
Albeit the
Last Chance Hotel.
We book in and pretend to be married,
Which is easy
Nobody seems to recall
To whom.
The sad, empty faces on the Central Line
Give no one a second glance,
The smog and the busyness envelop us
Into this new world.
Slowly we drink in the feeling,
Sliding in the park,
Turning our love roundabout,
Your smile reaches across the playground
Hand in hand we swing
Into the mood.

A Logue, Swanage, Dorset

GROWING PAINS

When we are together,
Oh darling grandchild of mine,
I feel like time is standing still,
Nothing could make us feel more sublime.

But recently I've noticed,
As time goes swiftly by,
That there's an interference,
In our simple, pleasant lives.

Now when we are playing,
There's an electronic beep,
You run off, at its beck and call,
You must hear it in your sleep!

Now I'm not one to moan,
And I don't really like to preach,
But can't you just turn that darn thing off,
And let's go down the beach?

Oh darling grandchild of mine,
Oh how I love you, Treacle,
But I don't like this modern nonsense,
What a shame that there's no signal!

Christina Baxter, Weymouth, Dorset

DIAMOND VISION

Well what can I say except that
They all made way for the lady in white.
Elegantly dressed, with her twinkling diamond brooch,
She soon put on a smile when the boats began to approach.
A thousand boats all played their part,
And floated on the heart of the Thames.
More and more the dark clouds began to gather,
And soon the rain began to pour.
The very next day the sun started to shine,
And everything turned out fine.
All kinds of music was played,
And the crowd's happiness was quite clearly displayed.
People danced and glanced at the Queen,
When she entered to take her seat.
At the end of the night a giant cut diamond
Was placed on a switch without a hitch.
A huge torch was then lit,
And gave out such a strong golden glow,
And amazing power was suddenly on show.

Ann-Marie Inman, Quedgeley, Gloucestershire

MICHAEL

I dream of you at night,
I see you in the light,
I call your name,
But you never reply,
You never said goodbye,
Your eyes were closed,
You were sleeping at last,
But I prayed you'd wake,
And tease me with your laugh,
I'd imagine, you were not really gone,
Soon to return where you belong,
You played a wicked game,
But you'd come home,
Tell me you were sorry for leaving me lonesome.

But you couldn't, for parting in death,
Waiting will not bring you to me,
But my love will last forever,
Until eternity.

I had a heart once, all filled with joy and glee.
But it has been destroyed, the moment you left me,
I never thought I could love, the way I love you still,
But I release you, and I shall let you go,
For I shall meet you in a finer place,
So Dearest Michael, I say until.

Sarah Bussey, Gloucester, Gloucestershire

NIGHT TIME

Night time at the beach
And at peace with myself
A light cool wind causes little movements in the soft white sand
The sound of the ocean's water is echoing all around
The stars and the moon lighten up the dark sky
A mystical picture and so impressive on anyone's eyes
Night time at the beach
A calming surprise

Amanda Vizor, Cheltenham, Gloucestershire

CAME THE DAY

I saw the host upon the hill,
The joy of life to fulfil,
The songbirds in chorus trill.

A blazon of colour to behold,
Before one's eyes a cloth of gold,
Oh, wondrous sight in the wold.

Came the day when a sight as this,
To blink an eye what joy you'd miss,
To stare in wonder at nature, bliss.

To walk in England's pleasant land,
Adventure unfolds like Alice in fairyland,
In awe at such grandeur by God's almighty hand.

This scene is likened to some passion play,
Would that I kneel upon this cloth of gold to pray,
That in my soul I'm blessed, came the day.

John Clarke, Little Witcombe, Gloucestershire

I AM UNDONE

I can't shift the cloud that's taken residence across my weary heart.
Despite the bombardment of distractions,
Inside I'm clearly falling apart.
Anger and frustration fire my soul,
Cursing the choices I have made.
Led by my heart and not my head,
Lies bare the bed of nails I have laid.
Contempt rears its ugly head,
Its shadow ever darkening my path.
A streak of viciousness I can't deny and I,
Ashamed in its aftermath.
Reel with my audacity yet nothing can cleanse my poisoned vein,
For that cloud, within a breath, returns to shroud my heart again.
Wishing dreams come true, hark hear reality laughing at my cheek,
So foolish my naivety,
For the path I so steadfastly and vehemently seek,
And I surrender, my fight is hopeless and I too tired to compete.
Dream shattered and I a shadow, broken and withered in defeat.
Each ugly thought, a tear in the fabric of morality I once wore,
Now ragged and threadbare,
With that contemptuous bitterness I abhor.
As I watch all those I love, reel from this monster I have become,
The tears fall and yet the anger rises once again,
For all I gave,
I am undone.

Rachael Hewett, Weston-Super-Mare, Avon

LELANT SALTINGS

Reeds, sharp as knives.
Jigsaw tussocks on the sea-soaked land.

Wrecked boats,
Jagged, gale-battered.
Broken.

Sharp white of egrets,
The grey of gulls,
A keening wind
Singing the winter in.

Sandra Hobbs, Bristol, Avon

THE SEA

Hurling winds persuade the waves.
Sulking gulls hide out in caves.
The rich sea air toughens the face,
Of the coat clutchers about the place.

Simple silence as night creeps in.
The horizon line is growing thin.
Sea sounds dominate dying desolation.
Bow, admire, marvel at Earth's creation.

The life, the world of the secret sea,
From Titan, to creature, to land and me.
So here I stand in awe and glow.
Beyond the depths of what I know.

Anna Gillingham-Sutton, Bristol, Avon

CHANGING SEASONS

In the summer of our marriage embraces held fast,
As we basked in the warm summer glow.
How good it was to be alive?
In love!

In the spring of our marriage, blossoms pink, ripe, in technicolour
Glory with daffodils dancing the theme of sunny amore and
Crocuses, tulips in a bouquet of ribbon colour.
My heart lifted high, forming to the sky,
A welcome band of rainbow,
Promising eternal, everlasting, ethereal love.

In the autumn of our marriage,
The russet crunch of days old mouldy leaves,
Clung to our well-trodden steps of old,
Beating down a familiar path.
The echo of my laughter sounding hollow against your soul.

In the winter of our marriage, the cold chills my weary heart.
Earth worms surge through the muddy depths.
A blood-red imprint of your head pressed tightly against my chest,
Love's light seeps golden white,
Through the torn-out shardy sheets,
Stark white innocence,
Gone!

Karen Rodgers, Chard, Somerset

LOVE, DESIRE, DELIGHT

Is love something the songwriters say
Will last forever and a day,
Or something that you have to search
And feel you have left it in the church?
Is love something which can turn out false
Like believing in Santa Claus,
Or something that we can't deny,
The main aim in life until we die?
Is love something you shouldn't have to say,
Or take for granted at the end of the day,
While if spread around with good intent,
May ease the way for those who consent?
If desire is for true love, and all that is true
Anything different makes one feel blue.
In that case there's not much one can do
Just hope the greater good will come through.
Delight is something you will find
Brings contentment to your mind.
Forgotten are those regrets,
They are labelled under a fallen sign
While pleasure seems to fill the air,
The world's alight, and full of care.

Norman Hutchings, Bridgwater, Somerset

FOOTSTEPS OF GIANTS

Walking in the footsteps of giants, she and he,
Pretending it's a skill, not a gift.
And the illusion holds water,
Because the holes are stopped up
With nods and deaf-eared affirmation.
There's no compunction in buying yeses,
It's expected, and the no's too specious to mean truth.
She cries,
For the anything world makes her want to sleep.
He forgets differently,
And no more effectively.
They plan numerous futures around
A supposition of a lengthy stride that eludes her
And taxes his forgetfulness.
A trial in parts, she passes the practice
Only to fall in the final furlong, and bang her head
Repeatedly as she dangles from his runaway stirrup.
Foundation laid by Gods of Form
And function ruin them,
Holding firm for years beyond count.
They crash atop the children who labour in their likeness,
A waste that passes enough time to call it a life,
A dream,
A calling.

Heather Bonsall, Bath, Somerset

RECOVERY

When crying she is calling out, hoping to exorcise the former grief.
When laughing she is almost shouting,
Wanting to be a part of something better.
She cries, she shouts,
She doesn't know how to compromise between the two.
What if she's numb?

When talking, he is soothing, hoping to calm another's grief.
When asking, he is probing,
Knowing that he is getting close to what he wants.
He soothes, he probes. He wants to know that she can say
Why she is numb.

When working he is listening, waiting.
While waiting, he knows that he is recreating a reality,
For whom, for her today, for him tomorrow?
She wants the same.
She wants to work, at what she knows, with confidence,
Unfettered, listening, reacting, writing and yet ...
What if she's numb and it's all gone?

He says not, she can now believe as much.
Two questions still remain.
How does he know and just how far should she go?

Gillian Saunders, Bath, Somerset

INSOMNIA

Footsteps alone that I hear echo.
Dampened streets gleam in the dark.
Velvet cover of inky blackness.
The quiet thudding of my heart.
It feels as if this very place,
Is now deserted, out of bounds ...
Walking, I am so aware,
Of ghostly spectres all around.
Rain that falls so soft upon me,
Keeps me company this night,
Forming diamonds, crystal droplets,
Shimmering through the old street lights.
Silence surrounds, as if breath held,
Yet broken by the faintest cry ...
Breath released, I hear it whisper,
Gently past me like a sigh.
Hands deep within my pockets warm,
My collar hunched against the rain ...
I love the peace of early hours,
Before life begins to stir again.
Glancing up, I see the dawn,
A glimmer of the faintest light.
Homeward bound, till I return,
Sleepless again, and walk the night.

Beverley Bōrresen, Staverton, Wiltshire

OUR ALLOTMENT

Blackbirds singing, pigeons cooing
Buzzards on the wing
Seeds need sowing, weeds still growing
On our allotment in the spring.
Spades and forks, trowel and hoe
Wheelbarrow, beansticks and net
A gardener's world is a constant one
With the weather, the slugs and the wet!
Rabbits and deer, muntjac and mice
We keep them out with fences and fleece
They all love our lettuce and eat lots of veg
Defence of our crops doesn't cease.
Summer's here, the sun's beating down
Watering becomes quite a chore
But all of our labours are so worthwhile
When we've carrots and spuds by the score!
Our shed's a haven, come rain or come shine
We've chairs to sit and relax
With birds in the trees and bees buzzing round
We escape the mobile and fax!
Whatever the weather, sunrise or sunset
No matter how hard the toil
Nothing compares to veg on your plate
That's just been dug from the soil.

Helen Scull, Swindon, Wiltshire

East
Anglia

IN A DENTIST'S WAITING ROOM

The next victim awaits the trial.
In his imagination he sees the Operator
Indicate the seat of artificial relaxation;
His whole body stretched out - neck extended,
No comforting arms to clutch,
A sacrificial offering to be worked upon.
He must suffer for the repair of his ivory castles
Which characterise his facial expressions
And on which his eating habits are dependent.
His fingers pluck at some loose clothing,
He is aware of the approaching needle
Which conveys the anaesthetising injection;
The vibrant drill assaults his ears,
An assistant ejects a water spray
Into every corner of his gaping mouth.
As work proceeds he prays,
Drifting into tranquillity as the sedative fluid
Enters into the area of his imagined pain
And warmth floods his whole being.
When the operation is over and consciousness returns,
A restored being arises.
He is no more victim but conqueror
Who can face the world
With his ivory castles once more intact.

Beryl Johnson, Cambridge, Cambridgeshire

AIRLESS

On a flat, grey sea,
The memory comes to me,
Of how we used to be.
It is my reverie.
I am not serene,
Just hollowed out.
I float like husk-wood,
Eaten from inside.
Your shadow casts its pall,
Over me and all my all,
Every brick of every wall,
My heart is airless and small.
The laughter mocks me,
If I recall the memory,
Your sour testimony,
That mimics tragedy.
And because I cannot see,
Past the way we used to be,
I am a flock of calamity,
Catastrophe on an open sea.
And as blithe as your recovery,
Mine is still in discovery,
Untitled sentimentality.

As it was meant to be.

Marc Hollis, Peterborough, Cambridgeshire

SEASONAL STAGE

The soft April breeze floats through blossomed trees,
Carrying the busy hum of the road.
Birds chatter and croon, late into high noon
In their own Mother Nature-bred code.
Soft-winged butterflies float low and then rise
Adding garnish to leaf and bloom.
Warm sun caresses my skin, the cool draught mingles in
Stirring up balmy scents and perfume.
The carpet of lawn, deep-set and well-worn
Layering various shades of green.
Rough terracotta pots, mark the carpet like knots
The colour of a sweet tangerine.
Clouds tumble in the sky, like a scenic spin-dry
Hiding the sun like a balmy eclipse.
Shade covers the scene, where spring has been
A wash of soft grey and charcoal felt tips.
I long for the time, albeit a crime,
When this experience is an everyday thing.
The garden becomes a stage, different scenes will engage
When summer flourishes from the awakening spring.

Karen Horn, Ely, Cambridgeshire

NOT OFTEN

Here's that rare thing, a glorious summer's day
In England's oceanic climes,
From dawn a cloudless sky sheds beams of light
Upon a landscape green and lush,
Results of weeks of rain and sprouting trees,
A slight breeze ruffles leaves and grass,
The local river sparkles in the sun
And lambs, now growing, gambol light
And frolicsome, the mothers bleating near.

Outside the village pub stand tables bare
Surmounted by a sunshade yellow,
Ready for lunchtime drinkers, foaming pints
In hand, with laughter and good cheer.
And on the village field move cricketers,
All clad in white and poised to catch
Or stop a sizzling ball the batsman's struck.
For some things never change, though nations rise
And fall, though monarchs die and regimes fail.

John Brown, Peterborough, Cambridgeshire

TRAINING FOR THE LONDON MARATHON

The trees and distant hills are crystal clear,
As is the wind that cuts my legs;
The hoof-marks in the path are sharp and hard,
The puddles shine with icy coats.

Crisp grass, crisp wind, hard earth and icy quiet,
The hard and glorious winter day-start.

The moon stands white and proud,
Beckoning the sun across an empty sky.
No clouds,
No sound,
Save the early song of a lonely bird,
And the plod of my footfall as I run.

Ann Barnes, Meldreth, Cambridgeshire

LEAVES IN AUTUMN

I lost my balance
Leaning gently on you like a leaf
Before the wind brought down a
Fusillade of foliage
To spin you, pirouetting
Through your life
As if a dream had drowned you.

I floated softly to the earth
But you had gone
Down a deep, dark tunnel
Where no light would find you
And it took a long time before the
Peaceful landing
Crushed my hopes with footprints.

David Hill, Cambridge, Cambridgeshire

ANSWERS LOST AT SEA

There's a vision of a man lying on a bathroom floor
His hands are warm behind the locked door
In red he decided to deny what life had in store
If that was his future then he'd find something more

In a day's dream man cannot make himself rise
His mind on the ceiling with a world in the skies
He can't find life with an end though he tries
To be his own saviour and dull his last cries

There's an answer outside for man to find,
Drowning in the dreams that only died

There's a headlight creeping through the window
His closing sight shivers to receive the glow
For his final line he buries his voice deep below
To tell a crowd a lie when they refused to show

For the day to come and uncover man's reality
With that sun he's a pathetic shadow to see
In songs a poem is struck away from the misery
He created his fall in a call to finally be free

Conor Beales, King's Lynn, Norfolk

GREY PEBBLES

Grey pebbles, sea shells, sea weed, float towards barren land.
Ending dawn-beginning day, widow's weeds defy cruel breeze.
Weary hands clear sandy eyes - bent figure screams at frothy grave,
Dying rose drowns, thorns claw to survive the ocean's force.
Figure limps into oblivion.
Mermaids sleep in Neptune's arms.

Betty Fenton, Hunstanton, Norfolk

MAZARRON MORNING

Spain peace, punctuated by unknown noise,
A bang and a bump and the shout of boys,
Bottle in the street crushed and gleaming, the always gulls,
Gliding and screaming.
Shutter shade shakes, someone's awake.
First coffee taste, bitter and biting,
Slide into new day, exciting.

Seagulls are the screams of witches,
Cackle cacophony cracking the sky,
Cool pool water gurgles and grunts,
Chitter chatter children,
Treasure hunts diving deep in the blue shimmer underwater,
Flashing bodies glimmer,
Rumble of traffic from sun-baked streets moving slowly,
The body heats, flip flops flapping over burning tiles,
Pleasure of relax, lazy smiles,
Soon it's sleepy siesta time in lazy, hazy Mazarron.

Marilyn Lucy Worship, Norwich, Norfolk

FRENTEN BRIDGE

The blossoms gay
Pass through the forest of green trees
In long grass and tall grass
Toadstools strewn in their path

Hares and ferrets, they play
With dandelions in the breeze
And even old brown dormouse
Has something to say

Strands of litter lay spread
Across the feathery path
Solid trees and elders of the tribe
Preside o'er Frenten Bridge

Come the summer, the time shall be
Just right for summer games
And father time will leave his mark
On the rat and the old brown dormouse

John Armstrong, Norwich, Norfolk

LOVE, LOST

The flies penetrate a summer's day
To balance out the bitter tang.
Stuck in the honey we so lovingly prepared
With blackened truths and lost promises.
The sweltering glow will cement words.
But cracks will appear, as cracks on winter
Skin so deep, so honest.
Strawberry smiles will glisten on.
Later, as is so predictable the rain will
Cascade and we will stare lovingly
Through each raindrop that captures a
Single moment, a chilling reminder ...
The murky puddles will hide dark
Desires in their depths.
The open fire warms a reality,
So convincingly contrived.
The spitting logs agitate the mellow tone
And puff out dark smoke, struggling under such a burden.
The coals splutter and drown, taken by the flames.
The fire roars and is seen by all ...
Flickering in their eyes, the captivating blaze
Casts devils in the room.

Joanna Sach, Ipswich, Suffolk

OPPOSITES ATTRACT

So sat love and hate,
Both arm in arm
Watching the dawn rise

Love turned to hate and said
Your misery does fill the skies

Night came to fall and arm in arm,
Both still sat watching.
Hate turned to love and said not a word,
For knowing it was all a guise.

Hazel Thomas, Ipswich, Suffolk

AUTUMN AFTERNOON

The pale October sun peered out
While keenness nipped the air,
The countryside was bathed in light
And all-pervading calm;
The river murmured pleasantly,
The breeze teased flowers fair
In rolling, open fields - a scene
Of gentleness and charm.

But had a tempest struck the earth
And rent the sky in twain,
Should gales have blustered far and near
And raged o'er land and sea;
Had all around been overcast
And drenched with teeming rain -
It would have mattered not one jot,
For you were there with me.

John Harris, Bungay, Suffolk

REALITY

Reality holds and duplicity I can scarcely comprehend,
A sweet facade, mirroring the tender brush of a warm summer
Breeze, caressing, appealing and angelic.
Conversely, this reality, tarnished with distinct ambiguity,
Has an endemic ability to transform.
A sly, double-sided coin,
Both faces adjoined however decidedly dissonant.
My worldly experience condemns reality,
Has an uncanny ability to appear tyrannical,
Treacherous and pugnacious.
A sharp, unexpected bite, struck from an obscured cavern,
Cursed with constant, malicious dark.
A petulant predator, a relentless presence.
However, despite its unnerving proximity,
Remains assuredly malleable.
An expectant mould, never stagnant, willingly alert,
And eager for manipulation.
Carpe Diem
Do not allow reality to become a greedy incessant whirlpool
Instead, warp it for personal advancement.
Friend, not foe.
In my fervent opinion, if the world is your oyster,
Then absorb my aphorism, reality is undoubtedly
Your pearl.

Jasmine Ottley, Tuddenham, Suffolk

ROOKS

Tall trees with spangled light.
Tough brown trunks veiled with green leaves.
Untidy, large nests, twigs and bits of orange binder twine.
Noisy rook nursery. Big, black birds swooping and calling
While brown songbirds huddle in the thick, green hedges,
Crap all over my car.
Bright, yellow sun, yellow fields of grain.
Big, black birds swooping down like the artist's nightmare.
Rents torn in the painting,
Black holes rending the fabric of space and time.

Stephanie Davies, Woodbridge, Suffolk

SHED MANSION

I can't get you out of my head,
Like a river can't get out of its bed

,

ve said.

, us bled,

e Sayer, Newmarket, Suffolk

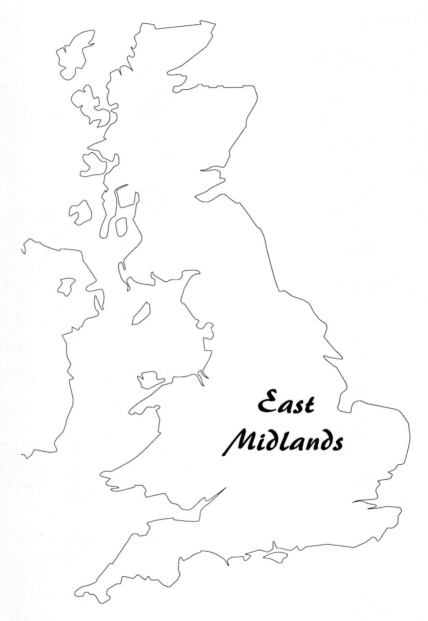

East
Midlands

PUBERTY

Between princess and woman queen
'Twixt mischievous grin and smile serene
Innocence and adult dreams
Stirring feelings still pure and clean
Flush emotions felt in flesh
Yet much too young to act on yet
The growth of feeling youth belies
The hint of woman in her eyes

Ivy Moore, Glossop, Derbyshire

SMALL CHANGE

As a child he loved fiddling with farthings
or hot-handling ha'pennies for their potential.
A farthing bought two chewy sweets
a ha'penny - bubblegum.
He coveted threepenny bits.

But now the change has changed
and so has he.
His saltglaze sight deals poorly with small things.
He hates appearing slow,
prefers to proffer notes or thick-cut pounds,
not querying his change.

He's seen old people offer
wallets, moneyed handfuls,
but feels they've lost the plot.
He visits town,
comes back with pockets stuffed with jingling coins.

Glen Mulliner, Belper, Derbyshire

SLENDER DREAMS IN SLUMBER

Standing tall for centuries
Hear the song of my green flags jingle.
I have watched you
Young and old, sweet and mean,
Whistling under my old branch trees.
Oblivious, you stand, you fall.
You whisper secrets, trivial and deep.
I sleep. Sleep on in an elder slumber
As the centuries jangle past,
Trying to draw my attention but they fail,
All the same, I watch you sail away.
After your dreams, some distant paradise.
I want for nothing, slender dreams in slumber,
Tall I stand, I watch you go,
But still you come. You want more.
The view I've watched for centuries in your sights,
And your eyes - greedy - seize the prize,
And I fall. Curving toward the Earth I bound for so long.
Come near me, gentle human,
Watch me fall.

Emily Thomas, Youlgreave, Derbyshire

LONDON WALK

On quiet streets of cobbled stone,
Your feet could gently wander,
Your eyes fixed high, on clouds and sky,
Freely you could ponder.
Yet on King's Road or Oxford Street,
Such serenity you squander.
For here your steps increase in speed,
Your eyes stay locked ahead,
On destination, determination in your brow, unsaid.

You call this stride your London Walk, and say so with a smile.
For a city girl you cover fast, an English country mile.

Sam Monaghan, Hope Valley, Derbyshire

SETTING THE SCENE

Ancient civilisations long past wilting
Ports defunked through rivers silting
Romantic ruins earthquake tilting.

Stone semi-circular seats raking
Greek comedy, tragedy, satire entertaining
Ghosts of bygone relics quaking.

Fallen columns and temples tumble
A mosaic floor survives Earth's rumble
Race after race rule, then stumble.

Human endeavours beyond imagining
Earth's past mysteries still unravelling
Heart and mind forever travelling.

Gillian Hartley, Repton, Derbyshire

AUTUMN

The rays of the setting sun
Smear the evening sky with
A fusion of vermillion and gold
Reflected in windows facing west
Above the guttering
Sparrows and housemartins
Chirp, chatter and squabble
Busy settling for the night
In virginia creeper
Which clings to walls and eaves
Crimson in its autumn glory
Herald of a dying season

Julia Richdale-Ellis, Alvaston, Derbyshire

WOLFGANG

Salzburg gave birth to a composer, a musician
A Wolfgang Amadeus Mozart, music was his mission
Symphony after symphony he did write
From being a boy to being famous he found delight
Born in 1756 Austria, his father Leopold a musician minor
Seventeen operas in a lifetime, his compositions got finer
First proposing to Constanze's sister who rejected his suit
His marriage was happy down to his cause root
Playing at aged three, a prodigy to the violin
Playing music to people who would be smiling
Sonatas and string quartets, his skills manifest
HIs music shone, bright and some were saddest
December 5th 1791, Wolfgang did pass
His music being at the top, being first class
His music now impossible to replicate
But his music still fine, although it was ahead in date

Emily Hiley, Derby, Derbyshire

THE NILE QUEEN

O Lydia of fame and fortune,
Fabulous and magnificent,
Decked in precious jewels,
Sent to conquer, all men of the earth,
O thy Nile Queen, of strength and fortitude,
Sunbeams shine down upon your palace,
With the sacred eastern scarab,
The golden sphinx and the lion,
As you sail the Egyptian sea,
For all the world to see, as your slaves bow,
To a royal sovereign queen,
O'er the pyramids and sands,
O rarest beauty is unleashed,
For imperial Rome must wait,
For thy heart is priceless,
For thy is a royal maiden of heavenly spheres,
Underneath the moon and stars,
As you walk the Nile gardens of peace,
Dressed in white, gold, silk and lace,
O great woman of the stars of heaven,
Show your ancient authority,
While bedazzling the world,
O powerful Monarch rising,
Like a golden phoenix,
Your eminence, O Empress of the Nile.

James Cameron, Leicester, Leicestershire

MENTALITY

Sat in a bottle looking out,
Life goes by, what's it all about.
Emotions pressed to be extruded,
Must join in or be excluded.
Unseeing eyes don't seem to notice
Anything outside their line of focus.
Rushing here, rushing there,
There is no time to stop or care.
Life goes by, but does it matter,
Should the bottle smash and shatter.
For who will help, who will see,
Those released into the community.

Michael J Guerrieria, Narborough, Leicestershire

LIE WITH ME

Breezing through the dead ends
Hoping for that forgotten friend
Family, unknown, unfamiliar
Find this essence that I send
Soul, alive or dead?
A stranger to the living
Alone, not dead but not alive
Welcome and free, the invariable strive
So is it in the music of men's lives?
Is it in the continuous face of the young and tried?
Is it in the disingenuous smile of an old friend?
Or is it in the love of a patient woman?
Let it be in me, let it simmer and spill in me.
Let not the world and the unforeseen perfume of death
Be carved on my head before my final breath
Let it lie in me, hammer and nail
Lie with me.

Stuart Morton, Oakham, Leicestershire

ROMANCE

Once feeling transcends dreaming
Eclipsing greed in pleasure's need
Shameless romance, our first instance
Love is the creed, and love's the meaning

Once the moon pulls at my womb
I take pride in my womankind
Hours passed in subtle lusts
Once satisfied are gone too soon

Once the soul consumes the whole
Breathless love charged to move
All the kisses, hot and listless
Fortune proves as rare as gold

OC Keens-Soper, Leicester, Leicestershire

STORY OF LIFE

Life is a story,
And we each write our own.
We write without help,
We write all alone.
And we write it in pen,
So we can't rub it out,
And it's piles and piles,
We've written about.
Pages and pages,
Stack up in our minds.
Hundreds and thousands,
Of hand written lines,
Some scratchy and faded,
Others fresh, black ink.
Every feeling we have,
Every thought that we think.

Megan Wood, Melton Mowbray, Leicestershire

109

HWYL FAWR

A bitter day, February, wind slicing off the bay
Onto the hillside, the tall tower
Echoing images of Auschwitz.
People, dark-clad, queuing,
Stamping feet like Holocaust victims,
Waiting in the cold for the inevitable,
Shuffling forward at a silent signal to celebrate death.

Inside, reverent heads bowed, muted whispers, muffled sobs,
Flowers like cloudbursts of colour
Against the stark, grey walls.
Familiar words, too familiar to those
Of a certain age - spoken to comfort,
To reassure, to promise.

Heralding song, the organ's chords
Fade into a torrent of sound,
A tidal wave of words, sweeping away grief
With its momentum, a tsunami of belief
Rising to the rafters, borne by voices
Rich in faith, lilting the language
Of their bards, its legacy an aftershock
Pulsating through the air.
Emotional electricity powering the spirit
To face the future with its balm.

Maryse Smith, Lincoln, Lincolnshire

THE VISION

Dew-spangled trees stood sentinel still
As I walked through the woods at dawn.
Mist was swirling like drifts of smoke
And a fresh new day was born.
I paused by a mossy clearing, and
There in the sun's slanting rays
A nymph-like figure was dancing,
Bathed in a luminous haze.
Her face was radiant in ecstasy,
Her skin glowed softly, pale as milk.
Cobweb fine her diaphanous dress,
And her golden hair glimmered like silk.
Her delicate limbs seemed to float
Above the ground as she leapt with effortless grace.
Piping music blending with birdsong
Drifted from some secret place.
She saw me, then vanished like a will-o-the-wisp.
I called, I searched, but in vain.
Transient as a dream she had gone forever,
And I never saw her again.
It haunts me still that magical dawn,
When I watched in the shimmering air.
For one enchanted moment,
The dancer with the silken hair.

Barbara Donald, Scunthorpe, Lincolnshire

BEWARE YE TYRANTS

Pale, delicate petals, so battered and bruised
Glimpsed briefly, only to be trampled and broken
Persisting, clinging, tenacious weed of the wastelands
Relentlessly uprooted, hacked, burned and poisoned
And still its roots persist, dig deeper, and endure
In quiet corners, those pale shoots will reappear
And though it may but seldom blossom
The scent will drive you wild, and haunt you forever
Ye believers, wherever there is fertile soil, plant it
Nurture it in secret groves, spread its seed afar and
Beware ye tyrants, of freedom's fragile flower
For its thorns are sharp and will one day bind you all

John Shillito, Barnetby, Lincolnshire

CAPTURED

It was a misty moon
Frayed at the edges after the equinox
A bold round harbinger of night
Glimpsed through serried ranks of poplar trees;
Turned earth of harvest gleaming spectre white.

I was its captive
Out beyond that moon
Enveloped by the scene
Music of Borodin echoing wave on wave
The falling leaves
The dykes and shadowed dusk,
A painting
An evening skein of geese in silhouette
Again, the moon
The peace, the peace, the peace.

Suzy Holligan, Louth, Lincolnshire

JUBILEE STREET 1940

Whitewashed kitchen, smell of gas,
Preserving eggs in isinglass,
Black lead grate and home pegged rug,
Parsnip wine in big brown jug,
Smell of bleach
Scrubbed table top,
Chicken's food in fireside pot.
Mantelshelf in green chenille,
Suet pud with orange peel
Family pictures on the wall
Aspidistra in the hall,
Outside lavvy - room for three,
Toilet paper - old ET.

Gillian Campen, Kettering, Northamptonshire

CLOSING CHAPTERS

Twilight waves
Bathe beneath the sun and moon, above and beyond
The veil that separates you and I
Our jail cell - our own making.

There may have been an upside
To the tragedy that became our love;
There might have been a chance to find our happy ever after -
Now we stand on opposite sides - far apart -
Living our lives ignorant of the chances we turned down.

Keep moving;
Keep breathing - oh,
Dusk is setting, and dawn is following but the brightness isn't.
Lost souls and unfinished stories - that's how our chapter closes.

Matthew Musselwhite, Northampton, Northamptonshire

PERIOD OF TIME

We're given at the time of birth
A period of time upon this earth,
The pages turn with each new day,
The chapters form along the way.

Each day and week, each month and year,
Given time with loved ones dear,
So much to feel, so much to give,
Such precious life for us to live.

Each day that dawns another chance,
To laugh or cry, or sing and dance.
No time for hate, no time for fear,
Each living moment oh so dear.

Audrey Smith, Hucknall, Nottinghamshire

CAVEMEN PARTY

There have been millions of years in the evolution of man,
So why do we still act like them, bare knuckled cavemen,
On the far left of the evolutionary scale?
When did we stop laughing at the everyday clown,
And started laughing when he fell down,
What gives us the right to judge another,
That is someone's son, someone's father and someone's brother?
Spread love like it is low fat butter.
Spread love to each other,
Like there is no other,
If this carries on,
There won't be any soul in any song.
Just around, around and around we go.
If this is my ride,
Then I am getting off.

Kenneth Gear, Kettering, Northamptonshire

THE LIBRARY

Eerily silent where
Robotic machines have replaced
Friendly counter staff.
Blue lights wink the way
To travel
To take out or return books.
Faceless screens, ever ready to rebuke,
Too slow, too late,
Take to the desk,
For human help.
Computers in quiet rows,
Wrap round the reading room.
No rustling,
Bustling, as glazed eyes stare,
At e-books online.
No chat, no fingering of pages.
Is print on paper
Redundant
Along with librarians?

Georgina Youdell, Nottingham, Nottinghamshire

OWL SAT IN THE TREE AT MIDNIGHT

Owl sat in the tree at midnight
Surrounded by the honey bee haunting
The spectre of the moon's dull light
Awaiting the sun's golden blue radiation ring.

The bees fled to the flower's deep aroma.
Pollen gripped the air in the bee's brain
While in the firmament shone the stars
And beside the river ran a steam train.

Owl saw a mouse running through its brain
And seized the moment from the midnight tree,
Killed the humble mouse while the bees
Created sweet nectar in summer rain.

Long gone is the owl now and the bee.
Long gone, too, the train, but the river
Still runs on through the wood to the sea.
Long gone, too, the moon's pallor, its dream.

Yes, now there is only the silence of imagination,
The silence of the moon, silence of the sun,
Silence of the wind in the cave's eaves,
Silence of the weeping eye, the silent tear.

Evan Gwyn Williams, Nottingham, Nottinghamshire

UTOPIA

Not a sound, not a whisper,
Not a murmur, not a sigh,
Not a car, not a person,
Not a bird, not a fly.

Just the sky and the mountains,
Just the sand and the sea,
Just the palms, just the sunshine,
Just the silence, you and me.

Christine Proctor, Mansfield, Nottinghamshire

CHERRY STONE DUST

Lay in sculptured desert, drowned in lakes of stone.
Acid temples of thirst carved light dark,
A mirage abandoned as we baked in,
As we smoked in, crystal air too hot to breathe in,
Too dry to make words sound in.
Did what was unsaid in that unmade bed,
Our unmade heads, that rouge hotel by the cliff,
The sea, stay with you as it stayed with me?
Pressed into air heavy as metal,
In dense red digital rust, cherry stone dust.
A liquid we swam through cold,
Weighed by limbs that froze, set, iced, aged,
Seized in a mould as we merged in crimson fires and furs,
Shot worlds from our fingers,
Wondered, wounded, but lingered,
On the shores we believed reason doubted,
Was deserting, was drowning,
In dense red digital rust, cherry stone dust.

Dean Geary, Retford, Nottinghamshire

West Midlands

THE CATHEDRAL

Solid and majestic
Soaring pillars, flying buttresses
The ancient edifice presides over the town.
Saxon and Norman,
Labourers, craftsmen, stonemasons shaped
Gargoyles, saint's faces, remote, aloof, looking down
On bishops, a saint,
The town-worthies, rich sinners
In redemption they lie, encased in stone.

Boy's face, angelic
The choir, robed and gowned,
The seniors solemn, pensive evensong flows out
To visitor, tourist, worshipper, atheist,
Student, scholar, the sick and the sound.

From the pulpit a blessing,
From the organ the sound,
Reaches up to the rafters where it rebounds
And fills every niche, every atom of air, every stone.
In the hush that follows a high child's voice asks:
Is God at home?

Ursula Mills, Hereford, Herefordshire

MOVING

Not for the first time,
We are leaving our house
Two months to go now,
No more long grass to mow
Floor to wash and sweep,
Fields of lambs that leap
From warm rural pastures
To cold suburban streets.

All must be packed
Book sorted and de-racked
Favourite plants potted
In the time allotted.

New friends to make
Old ones with hands to shake
Life must continually thrive
Wherever we decide to live.

John Kinross, Hereford, Herefordshire

NO THROUGH ROAD

A distant thoroughfare,
Suburbia litters the streets
Echoing concrete tramples the grass;
Congestion delivers solace in routine.
Scaffolding rescues daydreams
With coarse views angered by ignorance - will
Socialism ever succeed?
Crass minds deliver lectures that never work;
Communism needs an army to stop another revolution.
CND rallies the Left. Stop capitalism, philosophy argues the best.
Bloody-mindedness delivers the vote and moans at the result.
Celebrities do not understand who drives the headline
The public never surprises the tabloids.

Caroline Ferguson, Bromyard, Herefordshire

WHEN DOES LIFE BEGIN?

Does life begin
When that new mother holds her little girl,
And brushes her sweet smelling curls?
Or is it,
When that little lonely boy,
Finds a family offering only love and joy?
Perhaps it is
When that person who has lost her way,
Has found her place to stay.
Could it be,
When that somebody with empty hands,
Is finally handed God's golden sands.
Maybe it starts
When that man who has stumbled through his life,
Is declared husband to his new wife.
When does life begin?
When will I have that something special, the big win?

Tanita Keeble-Blaber, Oswestry, Shropshire

EVENTIDE

The day is almost over
As the sun sinks in the west,
This is the lovely eventide,
The time I love the best,
And from the east the moon appears
To give a different light,
Bidding the sun a fond farewell
Turning daytime into night.

Ivy Willets, Brunt, Staffordshire

I'LL BE THE SEA

These hands lie vacant, nothing to show
All my seas wave over, mountains of snow
Bring your boat back to me, hidden in the lake
A cavern of raindrops, keeps me awake

Throw peat on your hearth, trail crumbs to your door
Lay the lady on the player, and me on the floor
And tea in my teacup, words on my tongue
The rhythm of the mountain, the sounds of our song

Keep your bookshelves full, of fables and more
The smoke up the chimney, and the wolves from my door
Some food in the larder, bread in the tin
Some love some peace, and a little of sin

I'll pull the curtains, you make the tea
I'll be the whistle, through the leaves of your tree
You be the tide, I'll be the sea
And I'll wait for you, if you look for me

Corinne Marbrow, Edgton, Shropshire

SPRING

Dandelion clocks floating in the breeze,
Sunshine, birdsong and tranquil seas,
Olive green leaves,
Laughing in the sun,
As spring turns to summer,
I feel at one.

Josephine Bailey, Leek, Staffordshire

DIAMONDS

Being exceptionally unique,
Each soul a diamond, yet part of all,
Mind and spirits ceaseless invention, a call;
Our creations intention - in doing good deeds,
We sow life's seeds - so grows magic's inception.
If we can make a difference,
A realisation - in some small way
Do and bring some good - then we save the day.
Make a moment have true meaning, a purpose to be.
Open our hearts to the world, uniquely, we will see!
True magic is life's miracle, with love -
Then we will rise above!
Loves powers are us - life's diamonds,
Each one of us. Wakes imagination,
With every inspired sensation,
The sparkle of diamonds,
The light that twinkles in our eyes.
We are souls - spiritual beings,
In human disguise.
True diamonds.

Paul Holland, Stoke-on-Trent, Staffordshire

THE PROJECTIONIST

Grey and black microfilm
Ran through lamplight
Makes a pulsing
Fog, a throb, a hidden mob,
Whose breath creates a dusting

On fat velvet bats
Relaxed, beckon
Like a finger
Coax, then poke, find the note,
A crowd of hearts broken, linger.

Two blue moons in winter
Illume frost
Make it bolder
Sharp, the heart, bitter art,
A crowd of lungs a little colder.

Close and warm whispering mouth
Pressed on flesh
Halts resistance
Shivering, giving, truly willing
Inside your cinema of insistence.

Amy Dale, Meir Heath, Staffordshire

LOST SOULS

Odd boots in a cobbler's shop.
Two fish all at sea.
Rare Motown records.
Soulmates, you and me.

Pete Hubbard, Burton-upon-Trent, Staffordshire

MOTHERHOOD

To hold your brand new baby,
So soft and warm and sweet,
From downy head through perfect skin,
To tiny little feet.
My babies gave such pleasure,
Those darling little boys,
Growing, learning, loving,
Playing with their toys.
Toddling, running, through the house
Learning to climb the stairs.
Arms round my neck all sticky,
Kisses that still my cares.
School today, my heart stops
How can I bear to part,
Big boys off you go now,
While I hold you in my heart.
Now you're both grown and married
Each with a lovely wife,
Thank you, my sons for giving me
The most precious days of my life.

Jeanette McKee, Ipstones, Staffordshire

RAF LYNEHAM 2009

They were not meant
To come home like this,
Still and silent,
Carried on supporting shoulders.

This should have been a joyful day
Marching with comrades,
Bands playing, flags flying,
Not draped across their coffins.

Not long ago, as boys in school
They studied maps of far off places,
Mountains and deserts, vast and arid,
But no one noticed Helmand Province.

Those who loved them watch in grief
The slow movement of this sad quartet,
All their hopes destroyed,
All their expectations gone.

Time will not move for them.
Now is all there is.
They will remain
Forever young, forever loved, forever missed.

Marcia Phillpott, Rugby, Warwickshire

MORNING FROST

See the world awaken with the frost
And shiver as the bedclothes fall,
And curtains drawn apart
Reveal a lacy window pane,
Beyond which lies an opaque pall,
A bitter dawn,
A winter masquerade
In snow-white shades, a scene which dies
More quickly than it came.
A pale grey sky is broken
By some shafts of yellow light,
And rooftops now are glistening,
Their chimney stacks all iced.
Below, the tinselled boughs are still
And fallen leaves in heaps await
The melting of their pretty coats
In daylight's kiss.
The morning breaks, the picture is lost
And those who wake too late will miss
The beauty of the morning frost.

Jackie Smith, Rugby, Warwickshire

ROSE QUARTZ

For times when you feel wronged and out of sorts,
When you're distressed, feel low and all alone,
Then take up this pellucid piece of quartz,
Rose coloured, warm, translucent chunk of stone.
Its atoms sing to you: *Don't be afraid.*
The crystal lattice tunes the basic notes,
Trace minerals augment its serenade,
Which stifles vile invective in our throats.
It sings forgiveness - reconciles us all;
Brings peace and harmony to calm us down.
Its inner energy transmits a call
To shed the musty mantle we have grown,
The grand effect of all of the above
Lays down a base for unconditional love.

Dave Brough, Southam, Warwickshire

THE INSTITUTION

I like to get up at six, not seven.
I prefer to wear the green cardigan and not the red.
I never wear skirts, always trousers
But that skirt is not mine.
My appearance is important to me,
So why have you not brushed my hair?
You forgot to put my perfume on
And where has my ring gone?
Same again for breakfast.
Why can't I have bacon and eggs?
I drink tea with milk one sugar, not coffee.
I thought you knew that,
I have lived here for three years.

Rachel Stait, Sutton Coldfield, West Midlands

WERE I TO STAND

Were I to stand on the highest cliff
And have to jump a gap just too wide for comfort
And risk certain death against an uncanny wind
And an untied shoelace

Were I to stand on a busy highway
And have to cross both sides in a fog
On a winter's night with a dizzy head
And a busted zip

Were I to stand halfway across a choking desert
And have to finish the job on foot
With a leak in my flask and a rucksack to drag
And a hole in my pocket

Were I to stand and look at life
And have to live the second half
Facing unhappy thoughts and a broken head
And a hapless heart and a tasteless laugh -
and to make matters worse I can't find my scarf

I might just do it, if I were with you.

Stuart Patnell, Coventry, West Midlands

LIKE A BAD GRADE

Like a bad grade
You play on my mind,
You keep me awake every night.
You force my mind to abandon everything else,
You are my thoughts, my life now
Until I finally get handed the facts
Every possibility seems so real
I don't want to expect the worst,
But there never really has been a best
With the control in my hands,
I crumble in shame, I try so hard
To correct the mistake that was made,
I try so hard to alter it in my mind,
But no matter how hard I try,
The truth remains the truth
You disappointed me
You built up my suspense and then
You broke me.
I knew you were never an A student
But maybe that shows you
That cheating gets you nowhere.

Adeishe Hyera, Billesley, West Midlands

FELINE FRENZY

Crouching, groaning,
Swooning, moaning,
Fracking, fizzing.
Hacking, hissing,
Drizzling, drooping,
Whisking, whooping,
Swooping, snatching,
Stooping, scratching,
Flipping, fussing,
Rubbing, brushing,
Flicking, nipping,
Wailing, skipping,
Growling, howling,
Yowling, prowling,
Pouncing, announcing,
With a flick, a swash, a sigh,
Missed it! Flaming fly!

Alison Hodge, Stourbridge, West Midlands

MY FAVOURITE TREE

So graceful you stand in your place,
Elements of nature each day to face,
At peace, so quiet and still,
Until the winds your branches fill,
Then you sway to nature's tune,
In daylight or beneath the silent moon,
Your branches thickened by nature's rebirth,
You are the very salt of our earth,
I see your nakedness every winter time,
Like a skeleton upon the green to dine,
Autumn takes your looks away,
Nature always has her say,
In spring to dress you at your best,
Competing in majesty with the rest,
I can just look out of my window to see,
All your beauty in front of me,
Dressed in green with a golden flair,
I can only wonder at your splendour there,
So many trees, but you are the one,
To where my thoughts in the mornings run,
Watching you change shape and form,
Thanking nature for why you and I were born.

June McGuire, Coventry, West Midlands

FOR LOVE IS EVERYWHERE

Just any normal day really
We simply met
How life then soon changed
And all the world seemed good
We talked about the plants
And drifted towards them
Into a new maze of life content
Spellbound by the beauty
And breathed in the sweet perfumed scent
Whether it be fate or luck
For that I cannot say
But love surprises all of us
In truth each passing day
The paths you walk
Through the doors you pass
Sometimes there's no one there
But someone will appear one day
For love is everywhere

Christopher Barker, Walsall, West Midlands

A JAPANESE GARDEN

Maples crimson red
Shimmer in water's mirror,
Stones rise from lake's bed.

New hatched dragonfly
Holds her damp gossamer wings
Still on a leaf to dry.

Fragrant flowers grow,
Cherry blossom arches high,
Bamboo stand below.

A cool breeze disturbs
The stillness of the water,
Carries scent of herbs.

Tranquil pools reflect
Pebbles sunken, shot in quartz
The sun's rays detect.

Silent measured space
Left empty to discover
Nature's meeting place.

Sheila Barnfather, Wolverhampton, West Midlands

TREASURES

If it's treasures you want to find,
Then go travelling through my mind,
Discover magical gems, diamonds, rich fluorescent and dazzling,
Everything that's there is wild, fantastic and mind-blowing.
Crazy colours, right through to the core,
Bringing creativeness and ideas to the fore.

Grace Mayne, Wednesbury, West Midlands

SPRING

As the cool spring air
Blows against my face,
The sun is slowly rising,
Creating an amber glow
On the horizon.

The amber glow shines
On the trees
Casting a large patch of
Black on the dewy grass.

Bright yellow daffodils,
Sway in the breeze.
The sun is up now,
Rabbits are coming from
Underground. Spring is here.

Aliyah Begum, Birmingham, West Midlands

MOUNTAINEER

Breathe in thick air,
Take a while, just to stare.

Blow out the warmed breath into the frozen landscape of the sky.
I feel like I could step out to that cloud, I feel that I could fly.

The shape-shifting wind teases me to move,
It coaxes and cajoles,
Whispers that I have something to prove.

But I know my taunting friend too well,
And smile a little at his futile sways,
I push into his icy laughter and meet his stinging gaze.

Louise Tapp, Berrow Green, Worcestershire

THE MIDNIGHT DANCE

They danced together till midnight,
Beneath the starlit skies,
The moon above was shining bright,
Love reflecting in their eyes.
Music filled the air so sweet,
As in each other's arms they stayed.
Glad at last, they were able to meet,
Their bodies in time with the music swayed.
They did not want the night to end,
As they held each other so tight,
They knew both were more than a friend,
As they held each other that night.
But all too soon the morning came,
And they had to break apart,
Would things between them ever be the same?
Would they forever hold each other's heart?

Gillian Reynolds, Shard End, West Midlands

MOTHERS

I am yours.
A fact that has been repeated through the years,
In the pale sunlight and decaying leaves.
You are mine.

I asked you for nothing.
You gave me a life, a world, a name
Told me who I should be
In every gesture and word.
A daughter's life is never her own.
Every feeling, every thought
Is an echo, a mirror of what has already been.

Yet, as she sails away
On a broken heart, an undecided dream
Reliving forgotten memories;
A daughter forgets her mother
And, for the briefest of moments,
Is alone.

A daughter will disappoint,
And hate, and hurt,
To live her unchartered life.
But, when the storm begins,
She will return. Alone,
We are unwritten.

Rebecca Shaw, Bringsty Common, Worcestershire

CHINA DOLL

Postcard blue eyes, wild and antique
Wide and eerie white all around
Bambi
Soaked in grass flames and
Guitar strings

Stained string wound like clockwork
Ringlets and garlands, knotted and intertwined doll
Engulfed in African snow and star-crossed

Plump apple cheeks like smiles
Dimples of sweet sulky children
Cherub
Sparked in soul fire and
Warm breezes

Paper cherries sugared and sweet
Drowsy and dormant for now
Shy
Finger to your lips and
Silence child!

Lauren Stevens, Bromsgrove, Worcestershire

THE WOLF'S REFLECTION INSIDE THE GLASS

A middle-aged man stands naked
In front of a full-length bathroom mirror.
The reflection of a grey wolf glares back,
Bearing its yellow teeth.
From inside the glass of claret
The wolf's reflection stands proud and fierce,
Primal content, primal desire, primal instinct.
The wilderness of grey city
Scrapes through which he roams.
Marking his territory with violent scent
Retreating into grubby bars and dirty corners for violent sex.
A smile of dominance, twisted at the edges.
Words foaming from the pages of legitimacy without moral cause,
Such action is just Machiavellian virtue.
Pulling the red rose at its prickly stem,
Looking back from the wolf's unflinching glance,
Walking down the corridor,
Dressed as a wolf in sheep's clothing,
Dark grey Savile Row suits.

Natalie Brookes, Redditch, Worcestershire

North West

MONOCHROME

Really he wasn't dead, though in his heart it was said he had died
with the spurn of a lover, at least that's what I read - Red

Although not deranged, strange voice in head
screamed he would have to change, re-evaluate, re-arrange - Orange

Imagine Hell on Earth not Hell below, emotions all on show,
had to survive, force himself to be mellow - Yellow

No disgrace in crying, but had to be seen to be strong,
big man in this scene, but not that man he could have been - Green

Broken-hearted, broken man, broken down. Drowning in his own
shadow, desperately needing lies to be true - Blue

Over, just wants it over, searching for ashes of gold
in an undertaker's pot, leaving nothing but his ego - Indigo

Wanting to die, monochrome arc cuts the sky,
each shade darker than the last, leaving loved ones to regret - Violet

Alex Bell, Crewe, Cheshire

TO MILO ON HIS FIRST BIRTHDAY

Just as the colonel wrote of old,
And indeed the grand duke in his time;
We welcome dear Milo to the fold,
And celebrate your birth in artful rhyme.

A bright new star shines in our lives,
The twinkle in your eye so alluring.
You turn the dark days into light
With your smile and finger pointing.

Is it nice, little man? The question we ask,
And your response is so appealing ...
It makes us wonder what your treasure cask
Will reveal and what you're feeling.

The future looks good with you in our midst;
We long to see the outcome.
Art or science ... what will it be?
You are our millionaire, and then some.

Andrew Muncaster, Macclesfield, Cheshire

GOING TO THE ISLE OF MAN IN THE FIFTIES

The boats were bigger then,
And crowds thronged on from the Pier Head.
Tickets were first class or third class,
And those in first class had more shelter.
Crossing the Bar was our rite of passage,
Marking the leaving of the Mersey,
And entrance to the open sea with no more sight of land.
The crossings were often rough,
And the boat heaved up and down endlessly.
Some passengers threw up on deck,
But the old breed of Manx seamen cleaned up cheerfully.
Then, like magic, the blue hills of Mann appeared
Like a mirage on the horizon.

Now no-one hears the mournful ringing of the Formby light ship
bell.
Sitting in the lounge of the Seacat,
Insulated from nature,
You don't hear or feel anything anymore.
On the old Ben-my-chree or Lady of Mann
You tasted the salt spray; you felt the sea move under you.

Angela Johnson, Chester, Cheshire

MY SISTER

You were a year or two ahead,
You had the top bunk bed,
And more vocabulary than me.
You knew the layout of our lives,
The hopes, the qualms, the joys.
Your words spared me a while,
The trial,
Of thinking for myself.
I liked to have my cue from you,
The world was new.
I felt secure using your words.
I copied them,
Even when they did not fit,
The way I saw it.
The discrepancy
Did not bother me.
Life like that felt sweet
And quite complete.

Ruth Evans, Middlewich, Cheshire

ESCHSCHOLTZ, TRADESCANT AND DAHL

They crisscrossed the world from the west to the east
As far as the pale Taj Mahal,
Intrepid explorers in search of new plants
Such as Eschscholtz, Tradescant and Dahl.

They studied the habitat where these plants grew,
On sandy or clay soils or marl,
And made careful notes to record what they saw,
Did Eschscholtz, Tradescant and Dahl.

These efforts to learn and discover were crowned
With results that were far from banal.
Their memory lives in the flowers that were named
After Eschscholtz, Tradescant and Dahl.

Anthony Payne, St Bees, Cumbria

TERNS OFF THE COAST OF WALES

Turn and twist, you artists of the sky,
Move in union, as one on your palette.
Turn and twist, as on pointed wings you fly.

Gyrate your silken bodies, black and white,
Creating beauty with your twists and turns,
On the blues of sea and heaven in my sight.

Now you dive on rigid, flex'ed wings.
Beneath waves, reflecting sunlight bright.
While overhead the Irish sea wind sings.

Twist, turn and dive, you swallows of the sea,
Paint your canvas with your twisting flight.
Create your feathered masterpiece for me.

Jamie Smith, Stockport, Greater Manchester

UNSHACKLE

Whirling in the shadow with our clouded vision
Freedom within, use it well,
Reflective embrace, clearing perception,
Internal shadows expel.
Floating with spirit enhancing breath.
Bathing our internal being.
Clarity of connection emerges
Energises our soul freeing.

Catherine Lee, Atherton, Greater Manchester

SWORN TO DEATH

With cemented hands, we fall to vernal vines
Whose curving arms embrace us as downhill
Our folding bodies roll, the love entwines
Around our moss that never should come to still.
Uneven is the course - much seems amiss,
Leaves, stones and flowerets tantalise our balm
By keeping us from an endeavoured kiss,
While still we live by pressing palm to palm.
The sun and grass spin in our frames of view;
Perhaps time moving is in happiest hours.
We meet the foot: our product, lying anew,
Was yarned in ivy silk and wrapped in flowers.
Once more have we entangled limbs to die;
We care no less, but kiss at last and sigh.

Hassan Imran, Bolton, Greater Manchester

PHOTOGRAPH OF MY GREAT GRANDMOTHER

In the teeth of her husband's death, she leans
On the cabinet with its ugly drawer-handles.

She strokes her neck, the last place he touched her.
Clutches a fan, snapped shut tight as an unwanted telegram.

She has never met my gaze. Stares out of the window
In the direction of Passchendaele. She left me the dark face,
Her far-off eyes, her determined chin.

Rosie Garland, Manchester, Greater Manchester

ELEPHANTS

There are elephants stamping on the ceiling
There are elephants trumpeting through the walls
Elephants a-roaring and a-squealing
Every time Man United scores

There are elephants bellowing after midnight
And slamming doors at every time of day
With no regard for other residents' rights
Making their presence heard in every way

There are many forms of persecution
Noise pollution's one. Why can't you see
If we can't reach some kind of resolution
Your ASBO will not just be down to me?

Tanya Fernbank, Trafford, Greater Manchester

147

WE ARE BALLOONS

Children are full of air, they're free
And so let others lead their way.
But it's too early for them to see,
That they do not have to obey.

Life pumps us full of helium, so
We can slowly begin to depend
On nothing but the air and go
Wherever the wind does send.

Rosie Cooke, Rochdale, Greater Manchester

LAMENTATIONS. (Kaddish)

Had the evil priests of some hungry god of fire
Erased from living memory a race entire
Had its connection to this world abruptly ceased
Save for the ghosts that haunted a young boys sleep?

The small, the old, the weak and vulnerable
The pregnant and the lame
Piled high outside the shower blocks ready
Waiting for the flames

That would transport them up the chimney
Into a smoke-filled orange sky
Only to fall back down to earth as ashes
Like manna from on high

And in the morning an unspoken dread
Left that young boy wondering
Were any Jewish children left
For had not all been chosen
And singled out for death?

John Mcdonagh, Heywood, Greater Manchester

HOLES IN SOULS

Workers trudging to and fro
With no apparent place to go
Factories closed and gates locked out
Frustrations bubbling, lots of doubt

Miles and miles of official red tape
Employers knowingly make you wait
Time is on their side, you see
Nothing but crumbs for the ordinary

Vacancies here, vacancies there,
Truth is - no vacancies anywhere
Employment disappearing left and right
Demolition the only "productive" sight

The government, with heads in the sand,
Say, *We've no problems, it's all in hand.*
We will climb out of this recession.
Just tell it to the dole procession.

And when you realise there's nothing left,
Even though your skills, quite deft,
You wade on through waves of despair,
With an even more determined air,
You find the world is full of holes
But none as large as the holes in souls.

Brian Warren, Wigan, Greater Manchester

149

FORGET-ME-NOT

The room is tidied for another day.
Last light lingers, gentle to take its leave.
Dimmed are the calendar country gardens.
Eyes must strain to see sepia faces
Displayed in polished frames on oak dressers.

Drawers packed full of a lifetime's memories.
Jewellery, hat-pins, coins and pearl buttons.
Wartime recipes, love letters, programmes.
Photographs, those forget-me-nots of life.
Sheet music, played in concerts and classes.

Her breakfast cup is downturned,
Surrendered and accepted into the saucer bowl.
Every night, she heaves her body to draw
Red velvet curtains and switch on the light.
Tonight, her eyelids droop, she cannot move.

She steps into dreams of a young woman,
Laughing, dancing in a field of flowers,
Waving a friendly welcome, beckoning.
And she descends into night's deepest sleep,
Sighing a last, last breath into the room.

Elizabeth Hart, Clitheroe, Lancashire

BETTING FRED

As soon as he receives his wage
He's flicking through the racing page
Looking for that winning horse
The one that never does of course

He finds a name, decides to pick it
Fills out bookie's willing ticket
Convinced the mule is *hot to trot*
Upon its hind he backs the lot

The shot goes bang, the jockeys steer
Asses perched, above the rear
Sweating horses hurtle past
With Betting Fred's, a dead cert last

Betting Fred's stomach curdles
As the horses jump the hurdles
They gallop past him in a flash
Accelerating with each lash

They fast approach the winning post
Pray Father, Son and Holy Ghost
The jockey's off and lost his bonnet
And all Fred's money is riding on it.

Jane Thornton, Oswaldtwistle, Lancashire

WELCOME

The gentle rain runs from his eyes to the salty rivers on his face.
The thousand stabbing knives leave her as the sun's warmth grows.
The call of the startled crow mellows to a babbling brook.
The pair of doves behold the fledgling.
It's a boy.

George Palmer, Heysham, Lancashire

THE PICNIC

Morning sun slants through bedroom curtains.
Mother awakens, senses its message,
A day for a picnic.

Drowsy troops are marshalled, orders given,
Breakfast eaten in haste.

Provisions prepared, troops paraded for inspection,
Buckets and spades assembled, dog and car at the ready.
It's off to the beach, carefree.

Ten miles from home doubts fill her mind.
She needed to get home
Fast.

Husband, attuned to hormonal activity, surrenders mutely,
Drives home, foot down on accelerator,
Flirting with the speed limit.

House is still standing.
Panic over.
Grill switch at *Off*.

Anne Fielding, Ramsbottom, Lancashire

SANGUINITY

Your smile invokes my envy
Your voice voluptuous
I cannot fathom your resolve

Me and you in the blue lagoon
The blue of your eyes reflect the ocean
The taste of you is visceral

This isn't love
I am about to faint
Render me, sweet pain, render me

Yasir Hayat, Ashton-under-Lyne, Lancashire

WAITING IN THE CAR AT TAM O'SHANTER'S FARM

Drawing a big bole tree in the back of a fungi book;
Daffs full out, smoked with blackthorn blossom,
Sudden shoots of hawthorn,
All bright and tasty bread and cheese.

Half an envelope to write on.

Neil Young's bass line calls to a preening bluetit
Passing seventy year olds creak, then jump;
A bearded goth with bobble hat
Sashays and waltzes with his red-haired girl,
Even the pigs lift their snouts in rhythmic sways.
The maroon coated allotment lady with trowel in hand
Breaks into a jig.

Although, rock and roll can never die
The green Volvo in front just waits, not joining in,
Casting reflections of ivy leaves and a dirty snowball sky.

Judith Railton, Bebington, Merseyside

153

THE UNVEILING

The church stood clad in scaffold,
Dressed up in its new steel coat,
Waiting in the morning mist,
Cloaked in pride from an angel's kiss.
The old packhorse seemed to stare
With cut glass eyes and tender care.
While all the gravestones there below
Look on with love, the church they know.
The marketplace of yesteryear
With banners high, has no fear
The audience watch with bated breath,
Their church reborn, a fate from death.

Alan Withers, Lytham St Annes, Lancashire

RA CHALET

A silent evening,
As the flaming orb glides below the Clwydian peaks ends,
For nearby a local blackbird sings her sweet farewell.
A distant lamb cries mournfully for her absent ewe
As the pale, full moon looks down benignly.
Gorse blossom scents the evening air.
Thoughts of love for one, once present,
Fleetingly disturb my heart.

How cool the evening breeze this autumn season.
Wisps of cloud float gracefully over the pale blue sky,
While the silver moon impresses herself upon the tapestry.
Such a scene endows my spirit with a balm of content.
Whisper. Thanks to Him who made it all. *And it is good.*

William Potter, Liverpool, Merseyside

154

BIRDS

Purple doze:
A pigeon purrs. A slap of surprise -
Oh. He ups and goes.

Plumed lover
Plummets with aplomb - tumbles over -
Plump wing plover.

I sift, search
For stippled lark, uplift tipped as larch -
The chanted blue arch.

Leaving, a curlew.
Upcurved query draws cold curfew
Over a far purlieu.

Over the bowl
Of dark a flown silence - a stark avowal -
Hollow note of an owl.

Susan Ironfield, Liverpool, Merseyside

NEED

Why do we need borders,
Rules, regulations and orders?
Why do we need papers,
False news about backstreet rapers?
Why do we need entertaining,
By people not worth celebrating?
Why do we need so much cash,
Money that'll bring out a rash?

But what do we really need?

Do we really need each other,
Relationships and love from your brother?
Do we really need a home,
Not a house, just a place to not be alone?
Do we really need the time,
Or just a little space to call mine?

All of these things we think we need,
But how much of it can you associate to greed?
A man knows what's his and what's not,
But why can't he be happy with his lot?

Simon Haigh, St Helens, Merseyside

PONDER YONDER

I'd rather be a visitor
Than reside in Paradise
Where every perfect day is hot
I'd long for some rain
To bring on a cool change
And wash away my sweat

I'd only book a day trip
To explore the Garden of Eden
A sentimental stopover
For old times' sake
A testament to humankind's
Unconscious kindergarten
Listening to tempting commentary
From its bold tour guide: the Snake

I'd prefer to be a tourist
Than to live in Shangri-la
Future memories certain to be enchanted
By souvenirs of my brief sojourn
Instead of taking such bliss for granted
Where happiness is expected
Rather than earned

Yes, I guess I'll just stay put - not yearning but contented.

Aidan Alemson, Douglas, Isle of Man

North
East

A WHEEL FRIEND

My friend he has two rubber legs
And bones, they're made of steel
He lives off nothing but compressed air
And doesn't need a meal

His backside has a leather seat
His arms have rubber grips
His eyes, one white, the other red
For doing night-time trips

And when he's sick and has to rest
A punctured limb depressed
I put a patch upon his wound
And soon he is refreshed

What would I do without my pal
I've never seen the like
We've rode the whole world over
My friend the humble bike

David G Dickenson, Hartlepool, Cleveland

NAVIGATING THE SEAS OF THE SUN

Mercury rising, spinning like a top
Venus, pale and alluring never stops
Earth revolving desperate for its neighbour,
Mars, to satisfy its lack of resources;
Jupiter reflects its deep red spot while
Saturn's rings shine so bright
Uranus remains the butt of all jokes, a weary
Neptune's gloom is forever verdant
Pluto looks on decategorised, dogged and cold,
A Milky Way to another galaxy.

Television and science fiction novels ferment our imagination
Of distant planets and exploration of space;
Where alien life forms battle for survival amongst each other,
Developing the best and worst of human characteristics
That led to a race for profit, domination or slavery.
All stories of good overcoming evil, trade negotiations
And acceptable compromise for a moralistic audience.
But what would we do if we happened upon another life form?
Conquer or submit, vanquish or validate?
The answer my friends is still light years away.

Robert Reynolds, Seaham, County Durham

FEVER FLOATS

Throw it away,
Syrup to somersaults.
Nothing has changed. Night hangs
So low my eyes sing:
Tell me what you see in it.

I am a gift
Of teeth and blood and hair.
And now, crawling
Through shit
I am begging you.

We could trick the tightrope,
And be swallowed whole,
Letting the stars mould and peel.
Or lick the cylinders, tears fall white.
The final act.

Natalie Crick, Bishop Auckland, County Durham

THE DEVIL - ETHEL

Ethel, you are not outside
My shield inconsistently protects
I fought to keep you at bay
My mind inconsistently protests
Ethel, you're not far enough away
I feel you in my hands
Traversing my barriers
I feel me in your hands
Ethel, you're not quite banished
Unless a part of me is too
What remains when I remove
The part of me that's you?

Steph Acaster, Brough, East Yorkshire

SAD SONGS

Sad songs, they remind me to write
Ovulation of the thought, gestating our speech to the word,
Impregnation, increasingly giving birth to further thought.
How different, as in the olden days,
Men described fantastical feats of swooning,
And their lovers blushed with admiration, bosom heaving,
But I need the sad songs to remind me to write.
The thought grows into inspiration, a child's ideal,
With teenybopper words evolving thought into adulthood,
Now full circle the thought is aged and expires,
Leaving behind seeds of new thought,
Writing our history,
Then it can continue,
Multiplying thought beyond comprehension,
Still needing the sad songs to remind me to write.

John Liddle, Consett, County Durham

SONNET OF DANCE

You're here with me and that fact makes me feel like a king
For you I would give anything because you are my queen
When I think of all the places we will go and have already been
My inner joy takes over and I simply wish to dance and sing

Throughout my life a warming sense of familiarity you will bring
For the rest of my life as if in a dream
I now feel as if I can tackle any obstacle
Climb any mountain
Wade any stream
My inner feelings shown outwardly with a banded gold ring

I have laid my cards out on the table
Since we met I have known true love
And I know you feel the same
Our story will be no timeless fable
It will not fly through history like a dove
But when I think of love
Dance is the only name

Luke Bowden, Hull, East Yorkshire

AS I SIT AND WONDER

As I sit and wonder,
As I look to the skies,
I suddenly realise how time flies.
How we forget the important things in life,
And only think of ourselves.
As I sit and wonder,
And think of a world where nothing was bad,
And all was good.
I picture many things as I go through my mind,
However I seem to leave important things behind.
As I sit and wonder,
And wish I had remembered more good times than bad,
As I sit and wonder, I shall wish I had.

Freya Molineaux, York, North Yorkshire

SAVED

Revelations shatter me,
Bring me to my knees,
I'll try to find my saviour,
Some higher power,
I'm not certain exists.

Reconstructions of myself,
Needed to lift me from the ground,
To raise my faith in divinity,
This may exist now,
For me.

A resurrection of a new me,
Rising from the ashes,
Breaking from my former self,
My faith is now resolute,
I am saved.

Stacey Quinlan-Smith, Kingston-upon-Hull, East Yorkshire

ROCK OF MY AGES

Rock me baby - slowly,
Not when you're stoned,
Cos I need a rock, not a pebble,
Or a craggy, crumbling face
On my coastline.

Or when you've had a line,
Hoping to feel alive again,
Or petrified? I'll crumble.
Then brushing your dust from
My clothing - will walk ...

Leaving you to survive,
In yet another dive
I feel guilt-ridden, as though
I'd given you the smack.
So now I respectfully ask ...

As I can no longer find home,
Whilst I inject this dust,
That you rock me baby - slowly,
For now I'm the craggy face,
On the coastline ...

Sylvia Smith, Ripon, North Yorkshire

CATCH ME

Drinking hot chocolate with you
Is more beautiful
And more exciting than
Beijing, London, New York, Paris, Rome.
Because of our silent, unspoken promises,
Because of our hearts' lullabies,
Because of how I love your smile,
Because of how you love to laugh.

I wish to take a photograph of
How, for a moment, you shine
Brighter than the bonfire
We lit on your birthday.
I wish to memorise our out of tune
Songs, our laughter, your heartbeat.

I feel sick with butterflies,
As if I'm stood on the cliff edge,
Ready to fall.
Please don't catch me.

Rachel Glass, Scarborough, North Yorkshire

MY BED - MY ROOM

My bed is a field of flowers
I could lay on it, sometimes for hours
My room is daffodil yellow and it glows of gold
It gives me great joy in my mind, my body and my soul.

I love my room.
I love my bed.
They give me peace of mind where
I lay my head.

My bed is not large,
Only room for one.
I crawl inside,
The electric blanket is on.

I purr with delight,
Warm and cosy tonight.
I stretch out, warm from my toes to my head.
Oh, I do so love my bed,
I sleepily said.

Helen Weaver, Whitby, North Yorkshire

HEALAUGH

It is good to be here, beneath these wings,
Among these hand-me-downs and holy things;

Here where, flanked by figures of coloured glass,
We pass this door, we tread this ancient floor

On feet familiar with freshest grass;
Where the burnished lamp still burns undeterred

And the light is furnished with fragrant words.
It is good for us to break our fast

On this bread; this spread was laid to outlast
The years, our fears and feuds of reason.

Where rose and lily, poised on altar-stone
With dauntless grace, though frail as flesh and bone

Still hold their place, still field their roving roots,
And yield their fruits regardless of season.

Daniel Gustafsson, York, North Yorkshire

A JOURNEY TO NOWHERE

Away from green pastures, swollen sheep and well-spoken accents,
I paced, laden with a bag of dreams and other things,
Smoking skylines rose like phantoms,
Black windows spoke of toil and poverty.

The smell of alcohol swirled in circles
Down a path to nowhere.
Darkness fell, shadows formed, grotesque faces on grey, high walls,
I strolled through sinful streets and shameful alleys.

Red lips, false smiles, man-made golden hair,
Whiffs of cheap perfume, dazzling rude colours.
I paid with frozen hands and warm desire,
The waxen light mauled a smile on my dry lips.

Hands on a heart-beat clock stroked the hour,
Shrill voices uttered murmured lies through
Cracks and cold walls; sweetened air smelt of sour poison.
The cold air clutched at me like a lover.

Wheels squeaked, engines drummed;
I shut my eyes to a distorted dream of numbers.

Sonia Mander, Richmond, North Yorkshire

THROW THE FIRST STONE

He's been around the block, broke a few rules,
Lied to the 'rents about not skiving school.
He's taken much credit where not much was due,
And bitten off meat that was not his to chew.
He knows right from wrong, and what not to do,
But has to make sure other kids think he's cool.
So he picks better moments and waits for his cue,
To say something quicker and louder than you.
He smokes like a trooper, and swears till he's blue,
And he does all the drugs that the squares wouldn't do.

But you shouldn't judge this self-righteous fool;
Unless you're prepared to judge yourself too.

Mikey Bambrough, Ashington, Northumberland

SIMPLE BEAUTY

How come something so simply beautiful
Is in its extreme as complex as a logarithm?
The whole concept unravelling mysteries
Beyond human understanding
Anything that is beautiful is carefully tailored to be so
A painting created by hours of artistic talent
A poem mulled over in a poet's mind for eternities of time
Natural beauty, is there such a thing?
One might say flowers are so, it could be true?
They simply sprout up from the earth, relying on God's elements to
nurture their early growth
But someone must have created them?
Was it God's steady hand that guided the flower buds into petals?

Michelle Cadby, Alnwick, Northumberland

THE LEGACY

Soft summer sun slides under
Weary winter's snow-polluted blanket
As the Earth cries out for more,
Breathing heavily under the legacy
Of H_2SO_4.

Lean, leafless trees stretch out against
The bright red litmus sky
Their lifeless veins pulse no more.

Asleep? Perchance to dream?
Soft summer sun seeks, in vain,
Their dappled shades of green.

Yvonne Brunton, Doncaster, South Yorkshire

BENIGN INDIFFERENCE

Oft she turns her wrinkled face,
Pirouettes through starlit space,
Agitated her demeanour,
Ageing, legless barrelina.
Now and then she belches, spews,
Shakes and quakes and so renews.

All is cyclical in motion,
Life and earth and sky and ocean,
Living, dying, rising, falling,
Though to us it seems appalling
For, short-lived, to life we cling,
While nature simply does its thing.

Christine Stromberg, Sheffield, South Yorkshire

CHANCE ENCOUNTER

It felt like strangers
At a party,
Eyes which met
But shyly cast aside
Like stones into a pond.
I know every turn
Of your body
Yet felt
I hadn't touched you
In so long.
It was a wrench
To leave you there -
A loss
Made keen
By past familiarity.
Bereft,
I watched you
Walk away,
Empty arms,
Empty heart
And I was left
To fill them
With a smile.

Judith Sanders, Rotherham, South Yorkshire

PROMISE

You, a precious jewel
Shimmering blue
A bead of compassion, wisdom, extravagant flair
A burst of truth in a blurred, browned world.

You teach me kindness,
Comfort,
Painstaking, inexhaustible care
And, when pressed, a flash of pure rage.

Your unquestioning trust in your illusory companion
Speaks to the child within
The wounded, scarred and wounding child
Her companion the jagged sword-edge of pain.

But to you she can be kind
Your shifting moods inspire tenderness, not fear;
There is no threat evoked, no sugared oppression.
In my painful, halting limp towards wholeness

You are the promise I see.

Carolyn Jolly, Sheffield, South Yorkshire

WATER TRANSFORMS

Creeping over the sand bar
Isolating a private realm.
Piles of granite, speckled grey,
Softly furred with lichen growth,
Loom through rosy drifts of thrift.
Wraiths encircle the druids' stone,
Glimpses of shapes of ancient men.
Rising tide lifts slimy seaweeds
Metamorphosed to graceful strands.
Forests of thongweed, straight and slender;
Starry creatures crawl on sand.
Water hides jagged rocks
With teeth to tear at timber.
Ship-traps, not discerned
Till the crack of wood,
The screams, the taste of salt
And fear, deep in the bowels.
Now, in calm days, seals lie like slugs;
Humping laboriously over rocks
Slip and slither into the foam.
Tumbling, free and flexible,
As children rolling down hillsides,
Turning and twisting, in fish-rich
Wreck and wrack.

Jean Hepton, Doncaster, South Yorkshire

TRAFFIC LIGHT EPIPHANY

Pretty, purple petals
Catch my weary eye
While waiting at the traffic lights,
Feeling time go by.

Shock of beauteous colour,
Within the concrete jungle,
Lifts my mood; commands of me,
Crack a smile, girl, shake the grumble.

Today has been a good day
Slipping through it in my mind ...
Amazing, when you look for it,
The gold that you can find.

Among life's difficulties,
Troubled hardships weighing down,
Purple pretties, they remind, to
Lift my head up, lose the frown.

Val Bolam, Newcastle-upon-Tyne, Tyne and Wear

GREEN

Tiny raindrops cling to slender grassblades,
Vibrant ferns sway in shady woodland,
Tall trees display their fine fronds
While tiny yellow rosebuds promise a colour splash.
Springy moss sits atop the drystone wall,
A soft cushion of green to delight us all.

Judith Magennis, Bradford, West Yorkshire

I AM ALIVE

I feel the rainfall on my face,
The summer breeze, a warm embrace,
Healing sun shining bright,
A moon glow through the peaceful night.

I see the springtime flowers bloom,
Proclaim the end of winter's gloom.
Smell fresh cut grass on a summer's day,
See patchwork fields of corn and hay.

I hear birds singing their refrain,
Watch raindrops on the window pane.
Feel biting winter wind and snow,
See Aurora Borealis glow.

Sense the blood curse through my veins,
Break free from these binding chains,
Value all I have and strive,
To live my life; I am alive.

Paul Wilson, Newcastle-upon-Tyne, Tyne and Wear

MORT

Death is easy, life is hard
Every day's a struggle, I put up my guard.
My daily pain, and suffering commences,
As the morning ends, my eyes tense.
I wake from my heavy slumber, yawn and ache,
My muscles weak, and my head full of empty lakes.
I can sense my body's battle with itself,
The fight is almost over,
I'm not just going to be a sitting book on a shelf.
My energy is at its least,
My attendance to church is almost as much as a priest.
I'm happy to leave this heartless world,
To somewhere pleasant, perhaps full of twirls?
Live gives and takes, but most importantly of all,
Death is easy, life is hard,
Remember this now as you build your walls.

Samantha Holmes, Newcastle-upon-Tyne, Tyne and Wear

THE WATER'S EDGE

You always sensed its closeness, strangely beckoning.
Often almost threatening sounds.
The piercing symphony of countless gulls,
Thunderous waters pounding rock-filled inlets,
Silenced only in the darkness of long-forgotten smuggler's coves.
And then at night a restful, tranquil ocean,
Reflecting mysterious moonlight.
Swirling early morning mists lifting to reveal
Shell-strewn seaweed carpets with
Lonely figures on cliff-top perches, gazing outward
At distant steamers with eastbound cargo,
Lingering before disappearing from view,
Leaving only the shoreline below, incessantly bombarded
By the timeless hypnotic surge of the sea.

Christopher Craig, Halifax, West Yorkshire

177

SYRIA

A barrage bombards the pockmarked beach
Shelled mercilessly from beyond the shore
Snipers trigger death from hidden depths
We're hounded savagely by dogs of war

For God's sake, whoever that might be
Please save us from this murderous carnage
The slaughter of our innocent children
Fills us with despair and abject rage

How can these animals inflict such atrocities?
Who, on earth is friend or foe?
Government forces or terrorists?
Will we ever know?

Will they ever be brought to justice
To pay for their heinous crime
Or merge back into their lairs
Sandstorms obliterating any sign?

So the massacre goes on
Mass graves and misery unfurled
Will anyone out there help us
In this so-called civilised world

                    Ian Tomlinson, Leeds, West Yorkshire

INTERNAL COMBUSTION

When the dregs of the day
Settle like sludge
In the sump of the mind,
And strands of despair
Foul the rotor of progress,
Atoms of intent burn brightly
For a nanosecond, then congeal
To be spat into the exhaust
Of futile dreams.

This will *not do,*
Clean the points.
Crank up the engine.
Tickle the throttle,
And feel the sparks fly.
Neutral goes nowhere
So shift into high.
Start the wheels spinning
With fresh ideas,
New ambitions, more drive,
Steer straight ahead,
And make dreams come alive.

Patricia Farley, Keighley, West Yorkshire

Northern Ireland

WHITHER ARE WE BOUND?

At night when sleep seems so elusive
And my chest is pounding with regret
I sneak outside to my back garden
And light up a cigarette.

It's so, so late but I'm wide awake
And I just keep thinking life's a joke
And after every puff I offer the air
Yet another ring of smoke.

As I look up to the twinkling stars
I whisper, *Whither are we bound?*
But no answer comes back to break the silence
I can't hear a single sound.

Reza Ghahremanzadeh, Belfast, Northern Ireland

OCTOBER'S CHILD

The moon draped in a creamy velvet suit,
Dipped low and softly cried.
She could not wait any longer,
Had to disappear,
Had to hide.
Dawn stretched across
The skies,
Magenta blue and silvery red,
Rolled out with dignity
And with pride.
Trees, all clad in rustic robes,
Shivered with delight,
And gently sighed,
All in honour of you,
Christian,
New-born October child.

Paula Kennedy, Ballymena, Northern Ireland

ODE TO A YELLOW ROSE

Ah, give to me a yellow rose
That wets the tongue with lemon hue
That calls attention to its corner
Where in springtime spring flowers grew.

In its petals dewdrops nestle
Sparkling like the evening star
Causing wonder of relation
Both so near thus yet so far.

Comes the evening, petals closing
Sinking into sweet repose
Perfume hidden until morning
To bid temptation's gates to close.

So fear thee not my scene of beauty
I shall not enter thy domain
For I shall keep thee safe and nourished
In hope to see my rose again.

Peggy Galloway, Banbridge, Northern Ireland

Wales

NIGHT BEYOND THE COACH WINDOW

Darkling day to twilight,
Dusk settling in so soon,
Sun fastly setting between the clouds
Too thick to show the moon.
Glimpses of the skyline
Fleet past between the trees,
Each moment drawing closer to night,
Thinning branches moving in breeze.
Darkling sky past twilight,
Night bringing in full dark
With silence sitting among tired folk
Returning from the park.

Speeding on the homeland
Coach heads towards the town,
Villages lit in the distance,
The roads bump us up and down.
Glimpses of the skyline
Fleet past between the trees,
The night is here and darker now,
The air begins to freeze.
Darkling sky is hovering
Above us and all around
Beyond the coach window now misted,
But we are homeward bound!

Heather Phillips, Nantymoel, Wales

A SCHOOLBOY CRUSH

Because I don't see you ... I'm driven to drink,

But please do not worry ... it's only school ink,

To prevent ever again being parted from you,

Next time we kiss, don't use lipstick, use glue.

Douglas Peachey, Swansea, Wales

BEACH GAMES

Voices of children play in the darkness
As the swell of the tides
Gather the gales and crash
And hammer the sands

Bands of rhythm hand in hand
Dance and swirl the waves
As they push and pull at the shore

More, more, the children cry
As they play with the past,
Time's oceans slipping, skipping away

With each castle
Each turret
All vanished away

Janet Hughes, Aberystwyth, Wales

THE ACCIDENT

He lay like roadkill between two lanes
Broken.
Already dressed in black.
Helmet tossed aside like junk and dented,
Through the shield winked a crack.
That glinted in the sun.

Passers-by huddled together like weeds.
Trying to decide,
Is he dead? Or not?

I was oblivious.

I rested my head and smiled at fresh blossom and polluted daffodils,
As Dylan sang through the rolled down window.

And a cattle truck passed by.
Nostrils flaring, sniffing out the last scents of life.

Sian James, Merthyr Tydfil, Wales

LAST YEAR'S REFLECTION

The days came and went this past year
With no recall of much to say
But for many a salty tear
Shed on many an awful day.

With no recall of much to say
No memory to raise a smile
Shed on many an awful day
My tears flowed like the river Nile.

No memory to raise a smile
Neither hopes to make me feel glad
My tears flowed like the river Nile
I cried and cried, I felt so sad.

Neither hopes to make me feel glad
Nor a reason to sing with cheer
I cried and cried I felt so sad
The days came and went this past year.

Dave Gallivan, Swansea, Wales

ON DEAF EARS

I told you I loved you,
But it fell on deaf ears,
I never heard you say it,
Or was it my other ear,
The one that offers silence,
The one that came defunct,
For we are kindred spirits,
Perhaps in more ways than one,
Though, whereas you have two aids,
I presently get through on one,
Yet for you I would wish for two ears,
To hang on your every word,
If you will only say you love me,
Thus be the sweetest sound I've heard,
Perhaps we can grow old together,
See out the years in growing decay,
When I can no longer hear what you say,
Yet we can learn to lip read,
And signs and symbols too,
For you to say you love me,
And I, my true love for you.

Bernard Smith, Newport, Wales

ETERNAL THRONG

To multi-coloured halls we go
When bodies turn to dust,
As souls we travel back to you
When in your love we trust
As bodies die, we rise and fly
We never stop and wait,
For Heaven lies before us
With angels at the gate.
As balls of light we flit and weave,
Where boundaries there are none,
Across the rainbow highway
That's higher than the sun.
Our lives are mapped out for us
We have to prove our worth,
Our payment is our souls' release
When we depart this earth
To soar and fly unhindered
Of any mortal frame
On wings of love and angel hair,
No thought of gloom and shame
All others then will join us
When their time comes along
And we'll all live together
As one eternal throng ...

Linda Jones, Rhondda, Wales

ESCAPE

Escape.
A molten chocolate, honey-brown mixture of escape.
A spherical onyx held suspended in its centre.
Surrounded by waters the hue of maple leaves.
Two perfect ovals.
Twin orbs of vulnerability, anger, pain and gentleness.
Swirling, surrounded by clouds hewn from diamonds.
Colours that penetrate.
Almond-honeyed waters wash their depths daily.
Within, a part of, drowning willingly.
A delicious experience, saturating every pore of your being.
Out of your depth.
Mesmerising, intermingling tears and ecstasy.
Possessed, consumed by some unearthly force.
To memorise every part of his soul and burn it upon your own.
To hold him tightly, to be devoured and turned inside out.
An all encompassing feeling, twisting, never-ending.
A panoramic view that holds no equal,
Knows not its power.
Such delicious intimacy.
As though fire, an insatiable thirst with no desire to be quenched.
His eyes.
Twin pools of escape.

Beth Richards, Gwynedd, Wales

AFTER THE FUNERAL

It was the morning after the funeral.
The curtains drawn back showed some sun.
She put away the large teapots
And went back to a teabag for one.

She counted the plates and the saucepans.
She sat in her mother's armchair.
Looked around at all the glass ornaments
And wished that her mother was there.

She'd found in a plain brown envelope
A letter that seemed intended for her,
Wrap up the cutlery in muslin
And think about wearing my fur.

It didn't say that she loved her,
It didn't say that she cared.
It had been tucked behind wartime recipes,
So perhaps she should have left it there.

Jill Berrett, Cardiff, Wales

Scotland

LESSONS

Some things I learned when I was young
Lessons to list and file
Beware the man with the silver tongue
The girl with the tempting smile

The world is full of hurtful things
Unwanted woes and cares
And every pleasure trouble brings
Be careful of life's snares.

Wander high and wander low
But know before you start
In whatever direction you may go
The world will break your heart.

Harsh the lessons you must learn
Before you find the way
And enjoy the peace you have to earn
At the closing of the day.

The day you're born, the trap is sprung
We walk on ground fragile
So beware the man with the silver tongue
And the girl with the tempting smile

Bert Leitch, Glasgow, Scotland

NOT WARHORSES

A Kailzie horsebox, pantechnicon sized,
big as a Winnebago, parks beyond
our Lyne Water picnic table. Four
golden girls in body warmers jump down,
swing open the rear doors, lower the metal ramp
and unsnib the barrier gate. There follows a pause.

Then, hesitatingly, out of the womb
of darkness the horses come, a dozen of them, led
by their halters, one by one, placing their hooves
precisely. Carefully they clatter down the alien ramp
on to the sun-warmed tarmac, clip clop across the road
and swing through the open gate into their field.

Released, halters removed, manes streaming in the wind,
they gallop towards the hills. Two dozen scattered cousins,
browsing the slopes, stop grazing and race downhill
to greet them, whinnying and full of joy. Snickering softly,
these innocent, magnificent embodiments of goodness
nuzzle each other, standing neck to neck.

Norman Bissett, Edinburgh, Scotland

LINES UPON A FIRST ASCENT IN GREENLAND

We cannot sleep; how could we, when
All power of dark is stripped from night?
Instead we lie awake again,
Observing pale, spectral light
And rise when the hour has finally come,
And try to soothe our aching bones.
Thankful the first ordeal is done,
We chatter dead faux-cheerful tones
And tie our boots, prepare our packs,
Cook breakfast over tiny stoves,
Hoist numb weights onto tired backs
And, yawning still, begin to move.

The spectral glow of noble ages past
Awaits this band of travellers, at last
Descended from the peak as in a dream;
And finally, I know just what I mean.
Although our hilltop tracks have long since gone,
The glory in my head and heart breathes on,
Aroused by words re-enamoured to their cause
Which sweetly sing, defying common laws
And flow in triumph up the mountainside
Till bursting forth in streams of splendid light
They pour into the sunstreaked Greenland night;
And I lie sleepless, stunned by Greenland's might.

Sam Reilly, Giffnock, Scotland

MY CHILD

Raindrops fall like salty tears
Hitting window panes
And the heavens cry
So sweet a sound
Hitting our ears
And people laugh
When children smile
Hitting our hearts
Yet no-one cares
When one so small
Falls from so high
On their way
To hitting the ground

Kim Baillie, Edinburgh, Scotland

LIFE

We struggle for all our days
Why, oh why
What is it all for
We come from ashes and return to ashes

Throughout our lives we do our best
Giving, taking, donating, receiving
To make a world for us all to love in
Is it worth the hassle

Life is not ours to choose
The length we cannot determine
The good and bad we do
Is it all a sham, or a gem

Carol Habrovitsky, Glasgow, Scotland

A DRUM BEAT OF RED PAINT

Ben Bhraggie has the hump
of a narcissist on its back
I want to evict your effigy
Because they cannot
Eject you into standing stones
Or morph you into a cairn
in remembrance of them
Because they cannot
I'd like to shove your Jackson
Pollocked inventory
down your gannet's gullet
But I cannot
Instead, I'll factor into the equation
a drum of red paint
flung into chiselled cheekbones
It wasn't the shepherd's warning
But I, planting poppies
on blasphemy
Because they cannot
But because I can

Mandy Beattie, Wick, Scotland

ON THE EVE OF MUM'S 90TH BIRTHDAY

Beautiful birdsong in the lane
The first bluebells purply-mauve
Bursting forth into the spring day
Carpets of celandine and wood anemone
Spread beneath the tall trees of hazy green
And covering the very banks of the burn
That babbles deep blue reflecting
The bright high sky

I have yet seen but 60 such seasons
And ponder on being granted 30 more
How wondrous that would be
But should I not reach that happy state
I know how hard I've always tried
To appreciate each graceful moment
That I have been granted

Waste not the graceful moment with thoughts
Of how you used to be - nor yet how you might never be

Vivien Heather, Inverness, Scotland

CHANT OF JEALOUS PRIESTS OF ANCIENT EGYPT

Let us bump off Akhenaton,
Take him down a peg,
From the grandstand of his own self-dignity,
I heard this undercurrent to the third word pray
In an old Egyptian temple yesterday
Let us show Pharaoh no pity
Any way
Non-monotheistic locust
Let us pray.
And then
Before Amen
Let us beg
Let us make a conspiracy
To ensnare
Nefertiti
With her Pharaoh - unaware
In their Isis-new lunacy
To beget a seventh heaven
Upon set of sun-god-discus day
Let us pray

Valerie Irvine-Fortescue, Aberdeen, Scotland

SONNET TO SLEEP

How precious and how beautiful is sleep
Who comes, soft-footed nymph, to close the eyes,
And take her weary wooer by surprise
Into the misty mountains, wild and steep,
Or the cool caverns of the boundless deep
To lands of magic where the curlew cries,
And strange adventures fraught with smiles and sighs.
All this is while the stars their vigil keep.
On midnight expeditions we can dare
The impossible with brave and eager heart,
For there is something in that dreamland air
That makes our reason and ourselves to part.
Days may be dreary, yet this solace gleams,
We'll always find excitement in our dreams.

Ruth Miller, Fort William, Scotland

DARK DAY

Today is the dark day, the curtains are closed.
Mum and Dad panic, their voices rushed, hushed.
I don't see their faces, don't want to look close
At their sadness, distress, their loving hearts crushed.
I shrink way down low, to get out of their way
I lie down on the soft, round, brown rug
And tell my young sister it's not time to play
Pull her down with me gently, give her a hug
Her big brown eyes question as she struggles free
We hear the strange voices, some men by the door
Paramedics rush past us, I don't want to see
We feel the vibration, their boots on the floor
My fingers feel comfort in soft, shaggy pile
As my fear and confusion slide towards peace
My sister looks up at me, I shush her and smile
The dark day has brought our sick brother's release.

Victoria Campbell, Dundee, Scotland

ROUGH RIDE

White horses my gran called them,
spray-crested waves spewing into frothy foam across the firth.
Frolicking steeds metamorphose
to wild surfing stallions,
charging Camargue and Lipizzaner demons
whose power thrashes against our bow.
The vessel lunges after each crescendo
borne on equine fury.
Stampeding mustangs
resistant of break
carry us home in rampant rage.
When calmed
by some elusive whisperer,
they retire
to their stables of the deep,
tethered,
but ready for off
at the crack
of Aeolian whip.

Greta Yorke, Prestwick, Scotland

National Poetry Anthology

All aspiring poets never miss sending an
annual entry for the National Poetry Anthology.
Even if you have won through previously, and
had your poetry published in it, this free competition is always open to you. And as it's the
only big free poetry competition of its kind, it's
the first one you should put on your list to submit your work to. It's the biggest free annual
poetry competition in the UK. Around 250 winners are selected every year, each one repre-
senting a different UK town. All winners are
published in the National Poetry Anthology and
all receive a free copy of the book. Many of
these poets have never been published before.
Send up to THREE poems (on any subject)
up to 25 lines and 160 words each
(a blank line counts as one line),
by the annual closing date of **June 30th** to -
United Press Ltd Admail 3735, London EC1B 1JB
Tel 0844 800 9177
www.unitedpress.co.uk
One overall winner also receives a cheque for
£1,000 and the National Poetry Champion
Trophy.

Another £1,000 to be won

A poem about someone or something from your home town can win you a top prize in this annual competition. Anyone can submit up to three poems for the competition. The top poem will win £1,000 cash. There is no age limit and no entry fee.

"The poem can be about something or someone from the poet's home area," explained United Press Publications Director, Peter Quinn. "It can be descriptive, historic, romantic, political, or personal - anything you like, as long as there is some local connection.This competition is open to anyone and is completely free to enter - so what have you got to lose?"

Send up to THREE poems,
up to 25 lines and 160 words each
(a blank line counts as one line),
by the annual closing date of
December 31st.

NEW BOOK IS A BOOST
FOR BARNARDO'S

Don't you wish you'd written down some of the funny things
you've heard kids say?

Well someone has - and they've put them all in a book to help
raise cash for Barnardo's.

"Things Kids Say" is out now (£5.99) and half of the cover
price goes straight to the well-known children's charity.
This hilariously funny book was launched by actress
and TV celebrity Lynda Bellingham at a Barnardo's centre, and
it includes 130 pages of comical real things that have been
said by real kids - along with illustrations.

"The book proves that kids are by far the best comedians. All
the submissions have been provided by people from all over
the UK and all the 13 artists gave their services free," said
Peter Quinn, managing director of United Press, which has
launched the book.

"To cut out the middle-man and make sure that as much of the
revenue as possible goes to Barnardo's, we aren't selling the
book in shops. You must order it direct."

For your copy, send £5.99 (plus £1.99 postage & packing)
made out to 'United Press' to United Press, Admail 3735,
London, EC1B 1JB. £3 from every copy sold goes direct to
Barnardo's. Postage is free if you order two or more copies.

To order by credit/debit card phone 0844 800 9177.